Tom and Scott,

Continue enjoying golf
and life's adventures.

Best wishes,

Chuck Miller
"The Traveling Guy"

ODYSSEY...

"A long journey
full of adventures."

GOLFING
THE U.S.

GOLFING THE U.S.

REFLECTIONS ON A 50-WEEK, 50-STATE GOLF ODYSSEY

CHUCK MILLER
THE TRAVELING GUY

ISBN Paperback: 978-0-692-73143-7
ISBN eBook: 978-0-692-73148-2

Printed in the United States of America

Cover and Interior Design: Creative Publishing Book Design

This book is dedicated to the memory of my mother and dad, who encouraged me throughout my youth to take on the challenges of life in an upbeat and optimistic way.

It is dedicated to my family and friends who, although they thought I was a bit crazy, encouraged me when I told them of my plans to go on a 50-week, 50-state driving golf tour of the U.S. with plans to play golf in a different state each week for fifty weeks.

It is dedicated to my wife, Myrna, who continually assisted me and put up with my long hours at the computer writing and getting this book published.

It is also dedicated to golfers everywhere for their desire to enjoy the outdoors, to compete against others and themselves, and to play what I consider the greatest of all games.

Acknowledgments ...
and Special Thanks

Special thanks to co-hosts Bob Casper and Brian Taylor and to producer Dave Glauser of *Real Golf Radio* for giving me the opportunity to report weekly about "Places to Play and Places to Stay" during my golf tour of the U.S.; to the men and women of the Convention and Visitors Bureaus, PR agencies, and Chamber of Commerce organizations who assisted me throughout the year; to the hotels, motels, B&Bs, family members, and friends who provided me with complimentary accommodations; to the golf course General Managers and golf professionals who arranged for my 141 rounds of complimentary golf; and to TaylorMade Golf for providing me with a golf bag, golf gloves, and golf balls prior to heading out on my golf odyssey.

Many thanks go to Ghislain Viau of Creative Publishing Design for his cover design, book formatting, and his guidance and never-ending assistance as we worked through the multitude of areas needed to make my book a reality; to Pamela Cangioli and Kimberley Jace, my helpful and very patient proofreaders; and to fellow members of the Hot Springs Village Writers Club, without whose encouragement and guidance this book would not have been possible.

Contents

Introduction

In 1960, while bumming around Europe for seven months following graduation from college, I caught a bug that has been with me all my life. It has continually impacted both my short-term and long-term decisions and goals. It is the love of travel, commonly known as the travel bug.

Having been born and raised entirely in California, when I caught the travel bug I knew I wanted to learn more about our fifty states and about other countries, their people, and their cultures. I'm not sure which country I was in, nor do I remember which month it was when I caught the bug. What I do remember is that I decided a long-term goal would be to visit all seven continents, as many countries as possible, and definitely all fifty states.

By 2008 I had been fortunate, through business and pleasure trips, to have visited all seven continents and seventy-two countries ... but I still had not visited all fifty states. I began to make plans to do just that. Little did I realize that I would not only accomplish a visit to all fifty states, but I would do so by playing golf in a different state each week while on a 50-week golf odyssey.

My book tells the story of my year-long golfing adventure, which came about through a chance conversation with Bob Casper, son of Hall of Fame golf legend Billy Casper. I met Bob while flying above the Atlantic Ocean at about 35,000 feet in a Royal Air Maroc 747 on a trip to Morocco. I was headed to Morocco with Billy, his wife Shirley, and a number of American golfers to write an article about the Hassan II Golf Trophy, a tournament Billy had set up with King Hassan II thirty years previously.

I talked to Bob of my interest in visiting and playing golf in all fifty states. I asked about the possibility of reporting weekly on his nationally-syndicated golf program, *Real Golf Radio*, about golf in each of the states I would visit. Bob liked the idea and indicated he would discuss it with his co-host Brian Taylor. They discussed it and decided my fifty weekly reports would blend well with their fifty-week-a-year programming format.

Once Bob and Brian approved my weekly report concept, I worked diligently for over a year trying to get a company to sponsor my radio segment and cover my expenses. I spoke with and made presentations to national companies, including golf club and golf ball manufacturers, automobile manufacturers, RV manufacturers, national food chains, and beer companies.

I contacted anyone and everyone who might be interested in the benefits of being my sponsor, all to no avail. But, true to my approach to life's adversities, I didn't give up.

With Bob and Brian's okay, I decided to proceed without a sponsor and began planning an itinerary that would take me through all fifty states. I didn't know if I could actually accomplish my goal, but I damn sure was going to try. I began to plan my itinerary and pick the courses in each state that I would report on. Since not all golfers who would hear my reports would have the opportunity to play private courses, I decided that I would play only courses open to the public.

Over the years I had been invited on media trips by Convention and Visitors Bureaus, PR agencies, and Chamber of Commerce organizations. I understood their desire to promote their clients. I began to contact these types of organizations in Arizona, New Mexico, and Texas to explain the benefits of having me report about their areas and clients. I asked for and received assistance with complimentary accommodations and golf. With this experience, and my newfound confidence that working with these types of organizations three or four weeks in advance of my visit to their areas would work, I felt positive my goal could be accomplished.

Since I was going to have to pay all my expenses, I also realized it wasn't in my best interest to drive hundreds of miles in different directions to play courses in a given state. I needed to play courses that were in close proximity to each other. This dramatically changed my course selection. I began to choose courses that would be along the route I would be taking, which would be first through the southern states to avoid bad weather, then have me head north through the Mid-South and Northeast, then back through the Midwest, and then on to the West Coast. On January 8, 2012, I left my home in Vista, California, and began my golf adventure. It would take me to each and every state and last until December 4, 2012.

Come take a vicarious trip with me as you read my reflections on the courses I played, the people I met, the places I visited, and the good, bad, and ugly happenings on my year-long golf odyssey.

...and Away We Go!!!

It started with a rush, and it wasn't adrenalin. It was water rushing from a hot water heater that had broken. Water was flooding the garage. This was what I heard when I went to the garage at 5:30 in the morning to get a suitcase on departure day of my 50-week, 50-state golf tour.

What a way to start! Was this God's way of testing my patience for obstacles I might encounter during my golf odyssey? Was this a bad dream? Once I realized it was neither of these, I turned off the water to the house and called Sam Homant, the contractor who had done all the remodelling on the home my former significant other, Shirley, and I had purchased a few years earlier. I explained my predicament and he agreed to come over and fix the problem.

At about 10:15 in the morning, with the rushing water problem ready to be solved and my bags packed, I doubled-checked my car trunk. It held the clothes I would need for a year on the road; the myriad of informative books about golf courses and locales throughout the U.S.; two large, plastic file containers containing an assortment of office supplies I would need; my Toshiba laptop computer; two cameras; my beat-up but still usable briefcase; and two bags of cereal, cookies, and other assorted goodies I figured I would need at the start of my trip. And ... of utmost importance: my trusty left-handed clubs, the new TaylorMade golf bag which TaylorMade had graciously presented me, three golf gloves, two packs of tees, six-dozen golf balls, and the rain outfit which I had worn while on trips to all seven continents.

I closed the trunk, backed out of the driveway, took a few photos, said goodbye to Shirley, who would manage the house while I was on my odyssey, and I was off to Fountain Hills, Arizona, the first stop on my tour. While on the road for the next six hours, I began to realize the long-awaited day had come and my highly anticipated 50-week, 50-state golf tour was under way.

I was excited, not only about the golf I would be playing and the places I would visit during the year that lay ahead, but also the opportunity I had developed to bring awareness to the Wounded Warrior Project during my tour. Let me be clear about this. I was not then, nor am I now, officially associated with the Wounded Warrior Project, nor have I ever received any compensation from them. Although I am not a veteran, I felt strongly about what the Wounded Warrior

Project was doing to help wounded warriors who had fought in Iraq and Afghanistan. I wanted to give back in some way during my tour, and I felt spreading their message during my travels would be something I could do. During my drive I hoped that all the planning I had done in preparation for my tour would prove to be correct, all the while knowing that I damn well would have to be resourceful, self-sufficient, and able to adjust to new surroundings and challenges for an entire year. Did I have second thoughts? Sure! Was I going to let these thoughts stop me? Not on your life! I had planned, talked about, and desired to make this tour for so long, I wasn't going to let some mischievous mind games hold me back.

I was about to do something that, to my knowledge, had never been done before. That in itself was stimulating. I was headed out to play golf in fifty states in fifty weeks, and I was going to give reports each week on the nationally syndicated golf show *Real Golf Radio* about golf, places to stay, and things to see and do in the state I was visiting. For me this was going to be an exciting adventure, an opportunity to combine three of my passions: golf, travel, and people. I was pumped!

Arizona – "Spoiled in the Desert"

The natural place to start my 50-week, 50-state golf tour was Arizona. It was going to be a relatively short drive compared to ones that would come in the future, and it would be over a highway I had driven many times. A mere six hour drive from my home in Vista, California, including a stop for lunch, would start me on a journey I had been eagerly awaiting.

The first stop on my projected 345 days away from home, was Fountain Hills, Arizona, a lovely community only minutes from Scottsdale and Phoenix. Thanks to the Fountain Hills Convention and Visitor's Bureau, my first two nights on the road were spent at the luxurious CopperWynd Resort and Club, an intimate resort located on a ninety-nine-acre hilltop location overlooking the SunRidge Canyon golf course. It had been a long time since I had the opportunity to enjoy a fireplace in my bedroom or the type of luxury that CopperWynd offered its guests. It was one hell of a way to start. I felt very fortunate my golf odyssey would start in such an elegant manner.

My week in Arizona was jammed packed. After a marvellously restful night at CopperWynd, I got up early to play SunRidge Canyon. I was teamed with three Canadians who were in the Phoenix area for eight rounds of golf during a seven day "holiday." We had a ball.

SunRidge Canyon's fairways were in a light tan dormant stage. This was good news/bad news for me. It helped my drives run farther but made my fairway shots a bit more difficult because of the tight lies. Fortunately my home course, Shadowridge Country Club in Vista had somewhat similar winter conditions so I didn't have to adjust my game very much ... it was still hit and hope.

SunRidge's front nine played mostly downhill while the back nine headed back up the canyon. Playing the White Tees at 6,004 yards, the relatively wide fairways were receptive but the hard fast greens were quite a challenge. My adjusted 92 was disappointing especially since I went 10 over par on SunRidge's last six holes, known affectionately as "The Wicked Six." The uphill last six holes, two Par 3's, two Par 4's and two Par 5's, were definitely wicked.

Water was not a factor on the course as there were only two holes that it came into play. However, the numerous fairway and greenside bunkers, both left and right dog legs, and the course's hard fast greens definitely made up for my lack of concern about water.

The second round of golf I played in Fountain Hills was at Eagle Mountain. I had played there once before during a media event for golf writers and was looking forward to playing it again. I wasn't disappointed. Like SunRidge Canyon, it also had wide receptive fairways carved through and around canyons, but unlike SunRidge Canyon, Eagle Mountain's fairways seemed to feed errant shots toward the middle of the fairway. For someone like myself who seldom drives the middle of the fairway, this made for pleasant surprises.

Eagle Mountain also had only two holes where water came into play, the Par 5 10th and the Par 4 18th. Although I usually have trouble on water holes, I am drawn to them as they are usually more scenic and more challenging, particularly when water is close to the green and the pin placements leave little room for error.

The third course I played was the Pointe Hilton Tapatio Cliffs Resort's Lookout Mountain in Phoenix. On my weekly report on *Real Golf Radio*, I characterized Lookout Mountain as a "hybrid course." The first six holes were more like a parkland course with trees lining both sides of the fairways. The remaining twelve holes combined both a parkland and desert setting.

The course, which had recently become affiliated with Troon Golf, had long been a favorite of locals and guests of the Pointe Hilton. It wove its way through rugged terrain, and from some of its higher elevations had beautiful views of Lookout Mountain. Because water was scarce in the desert, lakes and ponds were really a non-factor. However, ten dog legs and an abundance of native grasses made good course management imperative.

My favorite hole was the Par 3 16th which I played from the Middle Pointe tees, the name the course used for what I considered the White tees. A quick look at the yardage book, which showed the hole was only 115 yards, didn't tell the whole story. Tee shots from the elevated tee box had to clear a gully of desert and cactus and avoid the severe slope in front of the green which more often than not would have a ball roll back into the gully. Also, tee shots had to be hit high enough to hold the narrow back to front sloped green. To add to my concern about the hole, just as I was about to tee off, my playing partners told me it was "the hardest Par 3 in Phoenix."

I hit a gap wedge to about eight feet above the hole and was told "you'll be lucky to have your downhill putt stay on the green." On that cheery note, I barely, and I mean barely, tapped my ball and then nervously watched it pick up speed on its journey toward the cup. As it was about to speed merrily bye, it caught the left edge, did a 360 and dropped into the cup for a birdie. I was thrilled realizing I had just birdied "the hardest Par 3 in Phoenix."

The fourth course I played in Arizona was Conquistador, one of two championship courses at the Hilton El

Conquistador Golf and Tennis Resort, Tucson's largest golf resort located just north of Tucson. I had the pleasure of playing with long time golf buddy, Bill Jones, his wife Helen, and Jack Rickard, a retired golf writer and former newspaper sports editor from Tucson. Golf to me is really a game to be played with friends. Such was the day at Conquistador. Bill, Helen, Jack and I thoroughly enjoyed playing the course's wide fairways, staying out of the desert, avoiding the few lakes on the course, and hitting to elevated greens

Since Bill was recovering from shoulder surgery, and had played only a few rounds in the past five months, Jack and I let Bill join us on the Whites even though he normally played from the tips. Bad decision! Bill shot a three over 38 on the front nine and had me in deep trouble on our $2.00 Nassau bet. Fortunately he tired on the last few holes of the back nine, and with two presses I won bragging rights and two whole dollars. As we played, Jack and Helen watched and laughed as Bill and I did our usual needling after almost every shot, something we had done for the more than 20 years we had golfed together. It was a great day.

All the courses I played in Arizona were wearing their winter tan. Green or dormant didn't matter, they were all enjoyable courses to play.

Off to New Mexico.

New Mexico – "Cold, Wind and Tacos"

When formulating my original travel plans for New Mexico, my first thoughts were to visit and play golf in Santa Fe and Albuquerque. However, having had a near-disastrous, life-threatening wreck when driving in the snow near Lake Tahoe a number of years before, I decided to avoid snow as much as possible and take the Southern route to play three courses in Las Cruces and one in the tiny community of Elephant Butte, an hour and a half north of Las Cruces.

Sonoma Ranch, Red Hawk, and the New Mexico State University Golf Course were the courses I played in Las Cruces. All three offered challenges I was ready to accept. At 6,100 yards from the Whites, Sonoma Ranch's rolling terrain, water hazards, and large, undulating, bent-grass greens—combined with a cold, howling, twenty- to thirty-mile-an-hour wind, made controlled shots a necessity. Fortunately, I was paired with Mike Elizalde, a Las Cruces local who knew the course. I have always enjoy playing golf with someone who not only has course knowledge but knowledge of the area. Mike was that kind of guy. We had a fun time, so we decided to play the next two days together at Red Hawk and the New Mexico State course.

While playing with Mike, I learned he was the co-owner of a well-known sports bar/restaurant, Ump 88 Grill. Mike and his partner, Major League Umpire Doug Eddings, number 88 ... hence the name ... took over an unsuccessful Irish Pub and turned it into a Las Cruces hot spot with a great atmosphere and specials every night.

When Mike told me about his restaurant's Taco Tuesday, it reminded me of spending many a Tuesday night enjoying tacos at my former home course, Shadowridge Country Club in Vista, California. However, when Mike told me the Ump 88 Grill served as many as 2,800 fifty-cent tacos each Tuesday, I had to see for myself. I arrived about 7:30 in the evening. Ump 88 was jam-packed with lines of people waiting to get in. I was told it had been that way since opening for lunch, just before noon. The tacos were good, the atmosphere upbeat, and the mixed crowd of college students, families, and groups of friends was a delight to observe.

Red Hawk was the second course I played. It opened in October, 2011, just months before I arrived in town. Situated on two hundred acres with one hundred acres of turf, fifty acres of planted native grasses, and fifty acres of natural desert, it was a links-style course ... with no trees, seventy-six large sand bunkers, and five lakes with water coming into play on eight holes. Like Sonoma Ranch, Red Hawk had rolling fairways and bent-grass greens and looked out at the Organ Mountain Range, so named because of the peaks that look like the pipes of a pipe organ. The surrounding desert, valleys, and Organ Mountains produced scenic visuals which made for a pleasant addition to my golf game. If the weather had been warmer and the wind calmer, it would have been even better. I didn't complain to Mike about the weather, although he and I both commented about it when we finished the round and adjourned to the clubhouse for a couple of beers. After all, it was January and we were playing golf.

My third golf game was played on the New Mexico State University Course, which opened in 1963. It was the home course for the New Mexico State "Aggies" men's and women's golf teams. The men's team had been the Western Athletic Conference Champion four of the previous five years. Over the years, a number of top players—including Rich Beem, Brad and Bart Bryant, and Tom Bryum—had played for New Mexico State, one of only a few universities in the nation that offered a Professional Golf Management Program.

The course was more of a parkland course with mature pine and oak trees lining most of the fairly wide fairways. Because the fairway grass was dormant and tight when I played, I got extra yardage on most of my tee shots. As a relatively short hitter, this was a plus. I felt comfortable on the greens, as they were smaller with fewer severe undulations than either Sonoma Ranch or Red Hawk.

Thanks to the complimentary accommodations arranged for me by the Las Cruces Convention and Tourist Bureau, and the management of the Hotel Encanto, my stay in Las Cruces was very pleasant. The hotel, southern New Mexico's only AAA Diamond hotel, had a historic atmosphere. It was filled with original photographs, vibrant colors, and numerous, one-of-a-kind pieces from Old Mexico,

Following golf at New Mexico State's course, I checked out of the Encanto and drove eighty-five miles north to Elephant Butte to play Sierra del Rio, recognized by *Golf Digest* as one of the "Top Ten Courses in New Mexico." Frankly, as I was driving I thought, "Why am I doing this?" as I was out in the middle of nowhere. When I arrived in Elephant Butte, population 1,300, I again questioned myself. However, when I checked into the Elephant Butte Inn, my worries went away. Although it was an older motel, the staff was extremely helpful, my room was comfortable, and the meals in the casual restaurant were quite good. Once again, I realized that small towns and older facilities have lots to offer.

When I played Sierra del Rio, located within the 1,000-plus acres of the Turtleback Mountain Resort, its numerous elevation changes, desert gullies, and well-protected greens proved to be quite challenging. Although the course had five sets of tees ranging from 5,060 yards to 7,300 yards, I once again chose to play from the Whites. Even with its wide, receptive fairways, playing from the 132 sloped Whites was all I could handle.

On my last day in Elephant Butte, just minutes from New Mexico's largest recreational lake, I spoke to the Women's Auxiliary of the American Legion about the Wounded Warrior Project. It was like preaching to the choir. The ladies of the auxiliary had been recognized locally, state-wide, and nationally for their outstanding work on behalf of veterans.

Following my presentation, I filled up at the local gas station and headed out to visit another site on my "bucket list," world-famous Carlsbad Caverns. Even though the caverns were a considerable way off my planned route to San Antonio, Texas, I'm glad I took the detour, as the caverns proved amazing. After an elevator descent to the Underground Rest Area some 800 feet below the surface, I took the Big Room Self-Guided Tour. I spent an hour and a half walking one and a quarter miles along a well-lit, mostly level, non-skid trail that wound its way through the cavern. I gawked at stalactites and stalagmites that began forming some 500,000 years ago. It was an incredible experience.

After my walk, I hopped in my car and headed for San Antonio, Texas, another day and a half and two tanks of gas away. It was a long, boring drive. A word of caution when driving through New Mexico and Texas: make sure you have plenty of gas and drive during daylight hours. Although the roads are good, gas stations and towns are few and far apart, and at night, the only light comes from the moon and the stars.

Texas – "Playing Where the Greats Played"

Since my dad and mother were both from Texas, I grew up hearing stories about Texas. As an adult interested in golf, I learned that golfers from Texas had become legends in the golf world. So, as I left New Mexico and began my long drive to San Antonio—the next stop on my tour—I was looking forward to my visit to the Lone Star State.

What I learned is that you don't just visit Texas. You become engulfed by it ... by the vast distances from city to city, the blasts of wind blowing across its desert landscape, and by the pride that its residents have for the state and its traditions. I began to understand all the stories about Texas my parents had told me over the years. However, it wasn't until I played the Brackenridge Park Golf Course in San

Antonio that I really became aware of what golf has meant to Texas and what Texas has meant to golf.

Brackenridge was a public course only minutes from downtown San Antonio. But it wasn't just a public course. It was one of seven municipal courses that made up the Alamo Golf Trail and was the oldest municipal course in Texas, having opened in 1916. It had quite a history, including hosting the first Texas Open in 1922 and twenty-one Texas Opens between 1922 and 1959.

Brackenridge was designed by famed golf course architect A. W. Tillinghast, who also designed the Winged Foot, Beth Page, Baltusrol, and San Francisco Country Club courses. Before playing, I visited the Texas Golf Hall of Fame, which Brackenridge houses in its small granite clubhouse; viewed the statue of famed golf instructor Harvey Penick outside the clubhouse; and learned that golf legends Walter Hagen, Byron Nelson, Sam Snead, and Ben Hogan all won Texas Opens there, and that Ben Crenshaw, Bruce Lietzke, and Tom Kite all won Junior Championships there.

Playing Brackenridge was quite an experience. My 83 from the Whites at 5,807 yards wouldn't have won me anything, but it was thrilling just to think that I had been hitting from tees, playing fairways, and putting on greens that the greats of golf once played.

At a little over 6,200 yards from the tips, Brackenridge wasn't a long course. However, because of more than 6,000 trees on its narrow fairways, and an abundance of fairway and greenside bunkers, it played much tougher than its 6,200 yards. It was enjoyable playing a course that was designed in the past, when shot shaping was more important than just bombing it from the tees, as is the norm on many of today's new courses. Position on Brackenridge was definitely more important than length, not only because of the abundance of trees, but because creeks and ponds came into play on eight holes—seven on the back nine alone.

Since Brackenridge was only minutes from downtown, it was easy for me to drive back to my hotel, take a quick shower, and still have time to walk over to the Alamo—which, much to my surprise, is located in the middle of downtown San Antonio. I watched the outstanding IMAX big screen documentary *Alamo ... The Price of Freedom* and toured the historic site. It was a most interesting and emotional experience to understand how and where Daniel Boone, Davy Crockett, William Travis, and the other heroes of The Alamo fought for thirteen days against overwhelming odds and eventually sacrificed their lives fighting for freedom.

The Daughter's of the Republic of Texas pamphlet I read said it all: "While the facts surrounding the siege of the Alamo continue to be debated, there is no doubt about what the battle has come to symbolize. People worldwide continue to remember the Alamo as a heroic struggle against overwhelming odds, a place where men made the ultimate sacrifice for freedom. For this reason the Alamo remains hallowed ground and the Shrine of Texas Liberty."

While in San Antonio I was also able to do something I had wanted to do for a long time. I rode on the San Antonio River in one of the colorful river barges that you see pictured in travel books and on travel shows. The narrated ride passed numerous restaurants with outside tables where tourists and locals were dining under brightly colored awnings. I enjoyed the ride and listening to the barge guide tell about the history of the river, how the lengthy River Walk was developed, and how the barge rides had become such a draw for tourists over the years.

While in San Antonio, a rain storm washed out one day of golf that I had planned. It gave me a good opportunity to do a bit of catching up, work on organizing the next stops on my tour, and do a load of laundry. Working in my rooms at my hotels—the Drury Plaza Hotel North and the Drury Hotel River Walk—was really quite pleasant, as both hotels were all-suites hotels with large, comfortable rooms. Happily, I was able to cut down on my meal expenses while staying at both Drury Hotels as all their hotels, and there are over 120 in twenty states, serve fresh, all-you-can-eat complimentary buffet breakfasts and complimentary cocktails along with an abundance of hors d'ouerves each evening.

The Drury Plaza Hotel North in San Antonio was a new, sleek, and contemporary hotel while The Drury River Walk was in a former bank, which opened in 1929. Drury Hotels bought it in 2003, spent four years and millions of dollars renovating it, and opened it as a hotel in 2007. With high,

high ceilings, stained-glass windows, and the former tellers' cages as the reception area, it was impressive.

When I left San Antonio, I headed northeast to Austin, the capital of Texas, where I was invited to stay one night at the Barton Creek Golf Resort and Spa, rated the #1 Golf Resort in Texas. It was easy to understand how it got its rating. It was in a beautiful forest setting, had all the amenities you would expect in a world-class resort, and had four outstanding golf courses, two designed by Tom Fazio, one by Ben Crenshaw and one by Arnold Palmer.

I played the Fazio Canyons course and was fortunate to be paired with Matt Higley, an Assistant Pro at the Fazio Foothills course. Other than the fact that he was forty-five years or so younger, had played pro golf until an injury caused him to give up life on the pro circuit, and that he hit the ball farther than I could follow, I found we did have one thing in common. Matt was from the San Diego area and had played my former home course, Shadowridge Country Club in Vista.

Matt was extremely helpful as we played. He gave me pointers as to preferred fairway locations off the tee, where to hit my second … third and sometimes fourth shots, and helped me read the tricky breaks on the greens. I wish he had also been able to lengthen my drives, hit my fairway shots, and sink my putts on the fast, sloping greens. He was quite a sticker.

While breakfasting at the Drury River Walk, I met a delightful couple from Austin. They told me a "must place for ribs and/or breakfasts" was Rudy's Country Store and BBQ, so I followed their suggestion and ate at one of the numerous Rudy's in Austin. The one I frequented served a good, fresh breakfast prepared by young, enthusiastic crew members in a fun atmosphere with red-checked tablecloths and peanuts on the floor. It was a casual, buffet-style restaurant that had a gas station and country store as part of its operation. It was definitely far superior to, and not like, any gas station/ convenience store operations I had ever seen.

Although they're mostly in Texas, I was told there were also Rudy's locations in Oklahoma, New Mexico, Colorado, and Arizona. I suspect there will be more to come if the rest of their operations are as good as the one I visited.

After breakfast, I filled up on gas and began my drive to Baton Rouge, Louisiana, which was going to include another long drive across Texas.

Louisiana – "Throwing Beads"

Mardi Gras is a great time to be in Louisiana as excitement is in the air. By sheer luck, after a long drive from Austin, my schedule brought me to The Belle of Baton Rouge Hotel and Casino during Mardi Gras. Located just a few blocks from the heart of Baton Rouge, The Belle, known for its 27,000-square-foot, five-story-high Atrium, was once the terminal for the Illinois Central Railroad. When I was there, it housed a restaurant, bar, and a number of meeting rooms. It was pretty remarkable.

Arriving in Baton Rouge during Mardi Gras wasn't planned. It just happened. Since everything I knew about Mardi Gras came from watching TV newscasters describe the raucous goings-on during parades on Bourbon Street in

New Orleans, I was ready to see it all for myself. When I read the Krewe of Jupiter and Juno was having their parade while I was in Baton Rouge, I was excited to see firsthand what a Mardi Gras parade was all about.

I called the number listed for parade information and by chance spoke with the parade chairman, David Villneuve. I explained who I was and what I was doing in town, and I asked for information about the parade. To my great surprise, David asked if I would like to ride on the Krewe's float and throw beads and doubloons to the throngs of people who would be lining the parade route. With great enthusiasm in my voice, I replied with a resounding "yes!"

The parade wasn't the wild spectacle I'd expected to see. There were no drunken damsels flashing their breasts to entice the bead-throwers, only throngs of excited men, women, and children happily begging for beads. After throwing hundreds and hundreds of strings of brightly colored beads from the Krewe's fancily decorated float, I got another unexpected invitation. I was invited to attend the Krewe's after-parade ball, which turned out to be a happy, friendly, celebration with lots of food, drink, and dancing. To say "I had a ball" at the ball would be a gross understatement.

At the ball, I was introduced to King Cake Vodka, a premium vodka produced, bottled, and imported from France specifically for Mardi Gras. It was not like any vodka I had ever had. It tasted like frosting from a luscious vanilla cake.

It was smoooooooth. After numerous toasts, a couple of locally brewed Abita beers, wonderfully delicious helpings of red beans and rice, a bowl of equally delicious gumbo, and a slew of Cajun dances, I thanked my hosts and turned to head the few blocks back to The Belle. As I was leaving, I was presented an unopened, brightly colored bottle adorned with the colorful and creative artwork of renowned Mardi Gras artist Andrea Mistretta. You guessed it—it was a fifth of King Cake Vodka. Although the vodka has been long gone, I still keep the bottle as a reminder of my first Mardi Gras and the hospitality shown me by David and members of the Jupiter and Juno Krewe.

After being in the parade and attending the Krewe of Jupiter and Juno's after-parade ball, I realized that, unlike the rowdy Bourbon Street parades and drunken parties, celebrating Mardi Gras is really a wholesome family affair. I also realized Krewe Members had worked all year raising money for the float, the beads, and the ball, and yet I was invited to be part of the festivities as an outsider. I was a bit overwhelmed by it all.

The morning after the parade and ball, nursing a bit of a headache yet anxious to play my first round of golf in Louisiana, I drove to The Island Golf Course, one of the nine courses that make up the Louisiana Audubon Golf Trail. The Island is located in Placquemine, one of the oldest cities in Louisiana and home to numerous antebellum structures. It was a short 20-minute drive from The Belle.

Unfortunately, golf at The Island was less than I had hoped for—not because of the quality of the course, but because of a lightning and thunderstorm. After putting out on the fourth hole, Dave Baron, my playing partner and The Island's Head Golf Professional, suggested we head for the clubhouse. Being a naïve Californian, I asked why. Dave pointed to the eerie, dark clouds that were rapidly approaching and said that, in a matter of minutes, we would be in the midst of a cloudburst. We hopped in our golf cart and headed for the clubhouse. Fortunately, we got to a covered rest stop just as lightning began to light up the darkened sky and thunderclaps began booming like bass drums at an outdoor concert, and rain began in earnest.

Since heavy rain was scheduled to continue for four or five hours, once there was a slight lull, we headed for the clubhouse. I'm sorry I was unable to play all eighteen holes, as The Island came highly recommended. With nine man-made lakes providing water hazards of some type on seventeen holes, it would have been quite a fun challenge. After thanking Dave, I set out for a quick sightseeing drive around Baton Rouge and then returned to the Belle for a catfish and French-fry dinner at the Belle's Shucks Restaurant.

Following dinner, I walked over to the hotel's casino, a Mississippi riverboat attached to the hotel via a long, wide corridor and gangplank. I wanted to try to beat Lady Luck. I was fortunate. I won a few dollars playing the noisy slot machines that graced the three floors of the casino and then headed back to my room to plan my next day of activities in Baton Rouge, which was to include golf at the Santa Maria Golf Club.

Located in a residential community of large brick and brick-trimmed homes, the Santa Maria Golf Club was one of the last courses designed by Robert Trent Jones Sr. In its early years, it was a private course. When I played it, it had become a municipal course run by the Baton Rouge Recreation and Parks Commission. Like The Island, it had plenty of water to contend with. Club selection and distance control was important in order to avoid the fifteen lakes and two natural waterways on the course. Fortunately, I was able to avoid most of the water. I say most because, with elegant splashes and a few choice words, I did donate a few balls to the water gods. Playing from the Whites at 5,737 yards, I still shot 85 and thoroughly enjoyed my day playing such a well-maintained and enjoyable course.

Following golf, it was back to The Belle to shower and get ready for a scheduled dinner at Boutin's, a local restaurant that I had visited years earlier while on a Mississippi River cruise. I met and dined with Lynn Boutin, the restaurant's owner. He introduced me to three of Boutin's specialties: crawfish won-tons, chicken gumbo, and grilled, farm-raised alligator, which came with a delicious remoulade sauce. I thoroughly enjoyed my meal and my conversations with Lynn. Listening to him was like taking a course in Cajun culture.

When Lynn excused himself to attend to business, I sat back and enjoyed the live band playing authentic Cajun music. While tapping my feet to the music, I remembered that Barbara Greco, one of our first Northern California Food Sales sales representatives, loved Louisiana and Cajun music. I couldn't resist. I called Barbara on my cell phone and had the band begin playing on my signal. I could hear her squeal with delight as the band played the music she loved.

Following dinner, I drove back to The Belle to pack for the next day's move to my next hotel, The Drury Inn and Suites. Having stayed at two different Drury hotels in San Antonio, I knew what to expect: a large, comfortable room, complimentary breakfasts, a happy hour with free beverages and hors d'oeuvres, free wireless and long distance calls, and a very helpful staff. I was able spend my next two days relaxing while making calls, sending emails, and planning in detail my next three weeks on the road.

When I left Baton Rouge and headed for Biloxi, Mississippi, I detoured a few miles to take a Cajun Encounters Swamp Tour. I was a bit hesitant at first as I got into their twenty-passenger "quiet boat" when I was told that, in addition to being home to raccoons, wild boars, snakes, turtles, black bears and a wide variety of birds, the swamp was also home to alligators of all sizes.

As we dodged around and under moss-covered trees and weaved our way through the back bayous and many coves of the Honey Island Swamp, I watched our guide point out alligators relaxing in the water and along the banks. Fortunately for this Californian, since most of the ones we saw were only three or four feet in length and quite passive, I didn't need a change of shorts following the two-hour tour.

After the swamp tour, as I drove to Biloxi, Mississippi, I reflected on my time in Louisiana. I had had a great five days and had checked off two items from my "bucket list": seeing a Mardi Gras parade in person and viewing alligators in their natural habitat.

Mississippi – "From Alligators to Bikinis"

As I began my short drive from the Honey Island Swamp in Louisiana to the Beau Rivage Hotel and Casino in Biloxi, Mississippi, I envisioned going from a view of alligators in a murky swamp to bikini-clad maidens around a hotel pool. I thought, "Wow, what a difference a few hours would make." Although it had been quite something viewing alligators in their natural environment, it was certainly much more enjoyable to contemplate viewing curvaceous, young, bikini-clad maidens lounging around a hotel pool. Unfortunately, I soon found out early February in Biloxi wasn't bikini weather.

When I checked into the twenty-nine-story Beau Rivage—a spectacular, Las Vegas-style hotel located on a wide, white-sand Biloxi beach—I was told it had been totally rebuilt following its complete destruction during Hurricane Katrina. I soon found out they had done a spectacular job rebuilding wonderful, modern rooms, excellent dining venues, and a well-laid out casino.

Thanks to the Mississippi Gulf Coast Convention and Visitors Bureau, I was given a room on the twenty-fifth floor overlooking the waters of the Gulf of Mexico. I also was invited to the reintroduction party for Beau Rivage's Biloxi Blonde Beer, originally made in the hotel's micro-brewery that had also been destroyed by Katrina, and set up for a round of golf at Fallen Oak, the hotel's private course. All this made me feel very much like a high-roller VIP … which, trust me, I wasn't.

After a casual dinner and a good night's sleep, I attended Media Day at Fallen Oak, which was being held in conjunction with the Mississippi Gulf Coast Classic Champions Tour event, which was to be held there the next month. Following the press conference, I was able to meet and speak with Tom Lehman, the previous year's tournament winner. As a golfer who had watched Lehman play over the years in numerous tournaments on TV, I was very much in awe to be able to spend quality, one-on-one time with him. Lehman was winner of thirty-four tour events worldwide, including the 1996 British Open, and the only player to win Player of the Year honors on the Nationwide, PGA, and Champion's tours. He was very open, congenial, and receptive to my questions. Speaking with him was an exciting experience.

Following the media event, I played Fallen Oak, a Tom Fazio-designed course open exclusively to the guests of the Beau Rivage. Fortunately, my day was complimentary, as the two-hundred-dollar green fee would have wrecked my budget. Although I drove my own car the eight or ten miles to the course, normally hotel guests begin their golf outing at Fallen Oak with a limousine ride to the course and star treatment that doesn't end until they are back at the hotel. The course, which opened in 2006, had been named "The Number One Course You Can Play in Mississippi" by *Golfweek* and rated in the nineteenth spot on the *Golf Digest* list of America's greatest public courses. It had wide fairways; big, deep, and strategically placed bunkers; and the smoothest greens of any course I had ever played. Although it was a treat to play such a stunning course, my game and score were nothing like that of the Champions Tour players who would play the course the following month in the Mississippi Gulf Coast Classic.

While in Biloxi, I also played the Preserve, owned by the Palace Resort and Casino. Designed with the environment in mind by U.S. Open winner Jerry Pate, it had lakes and acres and acres of native grasses to hit over and around, and hard fast greens with subtle slopes and breaks. In 2007, it was selected as one of America's Best New Courses. When I played it, it was one of only twenty-one golf facilities in the world to receive the prestigious designation as a Certified Silver Audubon International Signature Sanctuary. It was a course I would like to play again, but later in the year, when early morning temperatures would be in the sixties. My nine a.m. tee time had me teeing off when the temp was a numbing thirty-four degrees.

Following golf, I dined with Taryn Pratt Simmons, the Media Representative for the Mississippi Gulf Coast Convention and Visitor's Bureau. Taryn treated me to a marvelous steak dinner at Mignon's at the Palace Resort and filled me in on the area while we dined. I had been on the road for almost six weeks, and this was my first steak dinner. It was soooooo good.

When I returned to my hotel and made notes about my day playing golf at The Preserve, dining at Mignon's, and the trip of lifetime that I was on, I reflected back to words often repeated by Carl Hanson, a good friend and fellow golfer from California: "Life is Good."

The third course I played in the Biloxi area was The Bridges, located in Bay St. Louis, a few miles West of Biloxi. It was an Arnold Palmer course owned by the Hollywood Casino. I was told it was one of the most scenic courses in the area because of its moss-covered live oaks, magnolia trees, and sweeping views of saltwater marshes. Boxing fans may recognize the name Bay St. Louis as the location of numerous primetime TV fights over the past few years. The way I played the course, you would have thought I had just come from a brutal ten-rounder and lost. The course was great but my game was lacking.

Following my stay at the Beau Rivage, I drove a few miles westward to the small town of Waveland and checked into a comfortable and convenient motel with a long name: The Coast Inn/Barnacle Bill's Waterpark and Mini Golf Resort. Convenient was certainly the key word when it came to the following morning, as another Mardi Gras parade was forming on the roadway just outside my door. It was a long parade that stretched out for more than three miles and lasted more than three hours.

I was like a kid at my first parade. I watched the endless variety of highly decorated floats ridden by hundreds of costumed revelers of all ages throwing beads, doubloons, and candy to the enthusiastic crowds that lined both sides of the road. I walked up and down the parade route and talked with men, women, and children about their thoughts on Mardi Gras and the parade. As I spoke with them and watched the excitement from both parade participants and parade watchers, I was once again overwhelmed by the fact that Mardi Gras was family-oriented. Unlike many of the New Orleans' parades I had seen on TV, the Baton Rouge and Waveland parades I had been fortunate to observe were definitely not "booze and boobs" events.

Prior to heading to Mobile, Alabama—the next stop on my Golf Odyssey—I took a quick break five miles West of Biloxi to visit Beauvoir, the Home, Presidential Library and Museum of Jefferson Davis, the former president of the Confederacy. Taking the self-guided walking tour of the estate, which is a National and Mississippi Historic Landmark, was quite an interesting experience for me. As a non-southerner, I learned a great deal about Jefferson Davis and about his twelve-year stay at Beauvoir following the Civil War. Although the house and the grounds had been devastated by Hurricane Katrina, they had been sufficiently repaired to give me a good understanding of the home, the estate, and life Davis led there until his death in 1889.

Having thoroughly enjoyed my visit along the Mississippi Gulf Coast, including the opportunity to play three outstanding courses, I nervously headed east towards Mobile. I was worrying about my budget, as I didn't have accommodations for two of my next four days in Alabama.

Alabama– "The Trail Beckons"

Have you ever been homeless? Have you ever wondered how you were going to get through the next day on a very limited budget? I had never even thought about these types of questions until I was driving from Mississippi toward the Alabama border on week six of my 50-week, 50-state golf odyssey.

In the motivational presentation I give to students and young business professionals, there are two concepts that I preach: 1. *"It's a Mark of Leadership to Adjust"* and 2. *"Never Give Up."* I thought about these two concepts as I drove from Biloxi toward Mobile realizing I had no accommodations set for the first time since I left home on January 8th, almost six weeks earlier. I was definitely in a quandary, but

I was not going to give up nor was I going to panic. I was going to press on.

When I crossed the border into Alabama, I stopped at Alabama's Grand Bay Visitor Center, parked my car, opened the door to the Center, and gazed at the neatly lined walls full of Alabama photos and brochures. When I proceeded to the counter, I was greeted by a happy, friendly, smiling lady with a lovely Alabama accent. I explained who I was, what I was doing, and my predicament. She understood and made hurried calls to a number of motels. She obviously had great contacts as she quickly secured a complimentary room for me for two nights at the newly remodeled Holiday Inn Mobile West I-10. My anxiety over accommodations for the next two nights was over. What a relief.

When I got to my room, I checked my laptop and found my calls earlier in the week to the Drury Inn in Mobile and the Mobile Convention and Visitors Bureau had paid off. The Drury Inn had a room for me, which included their complimentary breakfast, evening cocktails, and hors d'oeuvres. And the Visitors Bureau had arranged two nights later in the week at the Point Clear Marriott Grand Hotel Resort, Golf Club and Spa, located on the eastern side of Mobile Bay. I checked out the resort online and found out it was a highly rated four-and-a-half-star property located only minutes away from the small town of Fairhope, which *Money Magazine* touted as one of the "Top 25 Places to Retire." Sure sounded good to me.

Having accommodations set for the next five days, I was able to take time to plan my Alabama itinerary, which included playing the Crossings at Magnolia Grove, one of Magnolia Grove's two championship courses. I was excited about the opportunity to play the Crossings as it was one of the courses on the Robert Trent Jones Alabama Golf Trail. The next day when I arrived for my golf game, I found out arrangements had been made for me to play with Paul Martino, the Crossings Director of Golf. This was quite a blessing, as Paul gave me pointers on how to play each hole and told me about other courses on the Golf Trail. Although I came off the course feeling pleased with my 86, which included seven pars and three double bogeys, I was quickly coming to the realization that my nine handicap was in jeopardy playing courses that were totally new to me. Frankly, I didn't care, because I was having so much fun.

The Crossings was a lovely course carved through a forest of hardwood and pine trees, quite a difference from the palm and eucalyptus tree-lined fairways that I was accustomed to playing in Southern California. There wasn't a house on the course, also different from what I was used to in California, just trees, rolling fairways, and slick greens. I did like the wide fairways off the tees, which suited my sometime erratic drives. However, the hard, fast greens with their subtle breaks and the course's two water hazards proved quite a challenge.

After hearing Paul talk with such enthusiasm about the eleven RTJ Trail courses, I was sorry my fast-paced schedule would not allow me to play all eleven courses. I also was sorry I wouldn't be able to return to Mobile for the LPGA Mobile Bay Classic, which was to be played at the Crossings later in the year. (Footnote: Arkansas' Stacy Lewis shot -17 to win the tournament by one stroke over Lexi Thompson).

My second Alabama course was Dogwood, one of two courses at the Lakewood Golf Club at the Point Clear Grand Hotel Marriott Resort, Golf Club and Spa, located on the eastern side of Mobile Bay, just minutes from picturesque town of Fairhope. The hotel, known as "The Queen of Southern Resorts," had an interesting history dating back to 1847 including serving as campground and hospital for the 21st Alabama Regiment during the Civil War, and as a training base during World War II. Unfortunately, hurricanes had also been part of its history. It was forced to close and remodel after hard hits by Hurricane Frederick in 1979 and Hurricane Katrina in 2005. Following Katrina, it was closed for nearly seven months, but reopened proudly following remodeling, which cost nearly $70 million.

I thoroughly enjoyed the Dogwood course. I followed my plan and played from the Whites at 5,855 yards, one of the five sets of tees which ranged from 4,725 to 7,504 yards. The course was quite challenging because of water on nine holes, eight on the front alone, and its very large greens, each with an amazing twelve different areas for positioning pins. I paced off one green and it was at fifty-two yards deep. Fortunately, I wasn't forced to make a putt of this length—but unfortunately, I did three-jack from forty feet. Dogwood was definitely a course with a great deal of character.

Following my round, I headed for the walkway along the sandy beach in front of the hotel. Although it was too cold for swimming, it was a delightful time to walk along the walkway, view the power boats and sailboats in the marina, and observe hotel guests walking, talking and playing with their families on the hotel's grassy knolls.

The next day, I was scheduled to play Azalea, the resort's second course. I didn't play Azalea due to a steady rain— wimpy native Californian's like myself don't play in the rain—but the course drew high praise from the couple from Maryland I was paired with on Dogwood who had played it two days before.

I found the hotel, which is listed on the National Historic Hotels of America, to be a perfect place to relax. With excellent restaurants and lounges, recreation and leisure opportunities, wonderful accommodations, friendly staff, and a location overlooking beautiful Mobile Bay, I decided I would like to stay and vacation there. But that was going to have to wait until another day, as my schedule called for me to head out to Tallahassee and then to St. Augustine, America's first city.

Florida – "Scratch Two off The Bucket List"

O ver the past few years, when thinking about golf history and golf legends, other than St. Andrews, there was no place I wanted to visit more than the World Golf Hall of Fame in St. Augustine, Florida, the oldest continually occupied European settlement in North America. When developing my travel itinerary, I made sure a visit there was on my radar. I am happy to say that during Week 7 of my trip, I was able to visit both the 450-year-old city of St. Augustine and the World Golf Hall of Fame.

When organizing my visit to St. Augustine, I was fortunate to have been put in contact with Florida's First Coast of Golf, the region's not-for-profit golf destination marketing company. They set up accommodations for me at the

Renaissance Hotel at the World Golf Hall of Fame Village and at The Fairfield Inn and Suites in St. Augustine. They also arranged a private tour of the three-story Hall of Fame and two rounds of golf for me.

Touring the Hall of Fame was an amazing experience. I was wide-eyed during the entire four hours I spent on the private tour viewing the lockers and busts of its 135 members; reading, seeing and hearing recorded comments and descriptions of each of the Hall members; viewing the more than 2,500 artifacts and memorabilia in golf's only co-ed locker room; and marveling at the special Bob Hope, Nancy Lopez, and Johnny Miller exhibits. It was a fascinating and educational four hours. The World Golf Hall of Fame should be a must-see for golfers of all ages.

After my tour, I walked out to gaze at the replica of the famed seventeenth hole at TPC Sawgrass, home to the Player's Championship. I was given a ball and a seven iron to see if I could hit and hold the green, which was almost entirely surrounded by water. My shot into a cross wind to the 137-yard hole avoided the water and landed on the green. Over the years, I had watched on TV as many of the pros hit into the water, so I felt pretty lucky that my shot held the green. Since I get nervous when playing for a two-dollar Nassau, it was scary to imagine what it would be like having to repeat my shot with hundreds of thousands of dollars on the line.

Although time did not allow me to play them, I did have a chance to view the two official on-site golf courses of the

World Golf Hall of Fame: The King & Bear—the first and only design collaboration and partnership between Arnold Palmer and Jack Nicklaus—and The Slammer & Squire, designed by Bobby Weed with World Golf Hall of Fame members Sam Snead and Gene Sarazen serving as player consultants

If you visit the World Golf Hall of Fame Village, you will have lots of restaurants to choose from. I decided to have dinner at Murray Brothers Caddyshack, which was owned and operated by actor-comedian Bill Murray and his five brothers. It was about a drive and a three-wood walk from the Hall and Renaissance Hotel. Besides being a fun place to visit because of the myriad of Caddyshack and Bill Murray memorabilia, it had excellent food … and drinks. The restaurant, its bartenders and servers, and definitely its patrons lived up to its fun slogan, "Eat, Drink and Be Murray."

While in northern Florida, which is marketed as "Florida's First Coast of Golf," the two courses I played were The Palencia Club, an Arthur Hills design located in St. Augustine, and The Golf Club at North Hampton at Fernandina Beach, just north of St. Augustine. The Palencia Club provided dramatic natural views of ancient oak trees and serene marshes of the intercoastal waterway. It was a difficult course with large hills and bunkers to play over. To give you an idea as to its difficulty, from the tips, it had a 74.5 course rating with a 142 slope rating. Needless to say, I wasn't up to that challenge and played it from the Whites, which was a daunting task in itself.

I was very, very fortunate to be teamed up with a young college student and member of the golf team at Flagler College in St. Augustine who was working at the club as an intern. He was a humble and well-spoken young man along the lines of Jordan Speith. He was also a tremendous sticker. If my memory serves me correctly, he was a +2 and his game certainly showed it. While guiding me through the course, and not playing in a competitive mode, he shot a two under 70 from the 7,100-yard tips. And this was with two or three lip outs that could have made his score even lower. Hopefully, someday I'll see his name on the leaderboard at one of the pro tournaments, as he told me "I want to become a successful golfer on the tour." I think he can make it.

The Golf Club at North Hampton was the site of my highest score, a discouraging 97, and that was with a number of X's. The course had very large, fast greens; an abundance of native white grasses; and ten boulder-lined, spring-fed lakes, which contributed to water on 16 holes. I was glad I had a bag full of balls as I watched eight times as my shots splashed elegantly, and not so elegantly, into the dark, blue water of the lakes. I was also glad course designer Arnold Palmer wasn't within earshot because I let out a few heck, darn, and phooeys as my game deteriorated on his course.

Golfweek had described the Golf Club at North Hampton as "The Seventh Best Course You Can Play in Florida." I didn't get to play the other six, but in spite of my score, I enjoyed testing my skills—or lack of skills—there, as it reminded me of some of the European-style courses I had played years before.

During my few days in St. Augustine, I took advantage of the opportunity to see and learn about the history of the area. I rode the Old Town Trolley, which took me to twenty-two, on-and-off stops all over St. Augustine. I enjoyed a visit to St. Augustine's oldest store, which was now a museum with live actors and spent time behind bars in St. Augustine's Old Jail, which was completed in 1891 and housed prisoners for more than sixty years. Originally built to resemble a fine hotel, it definitely wasn't one that I would have liked to check into. Starring out from behind the bars of the cell, I was reminded once again why I never want to go to jail. I can't imagine how prisoners survived that hell hole, and in fact, I was told that many didn't.

Following golf, I drove to Amelia Island, which was only minutes from the Golf Club of North Hampton. Arrangements had been made for me to stay at the Amelia Hotel at the Beach, located just across the street from a smooth, sandy beach and a funky local's restaurant. Having a desire to see the beach and try a local beer, I walked across the street and ponied up to the bar. Being the shy person that I am, I struck up conversations with a number of the transplanted northerners who had deserted the cold north for the sunshine and beaches of Amelia Beach. I stayed late, learned a great deal about the totally different and relaxing lifestyle they were leading, and then gingerly walked back across the street to the hotel. Another wonderful day and evening on the greatest adventure of my life.

The next morning, while reflecting on my delightful days in Northern Florida, I packed my bags and headed north toward my next golfing destination: Augusta, Georgia … home to, you know, that place where they give out the Green Jacket.

Georgia – "Augusta National... Almost"

A s I drove to Georgia from Florida, I was excited. My goal was to visit Augusta National, home of the Masters and the coveted Green Jacket. I'd been told that getting on the grounds of the course was an impossible task unless you were a club member. Being the optimist that I am, as I crossed the Florida/Georgia border headed for Savannah—my first stop in Georgia—I was convinced I could do it.

When I reached Savannah, I checked into my motel, the Thunderbird Inn, self-proclaimed as the "Hippest Hotel in Savannah." Inn-keeper Mark Thomas gave me a quick tour of the motel with its vibrant red, white, yellow, and blue color scheme. Having grown up in the Fifties, I enjoyed its retro look. I was given one of the large, remodeled rooms and slept like a baby until it was time to get up for my complimentary continental breakfast, which I topped off with two ... well, maybe three ... fresh and delicious Krispy Kreme glazed donuts.

Now that I was up, it was time for a half-day of sightseeing. I took the hop-on, hop-off Old Town Trolley and got a great understanding of Savannah and its history. Once the tour was over, I walked along River Street, which had more than fifty shops and twenty-six restaurants, including an old-fashioned ice cream store located inside the Savannah Candy store. I stopped for a cone. I had a tough time deciding, as there were forty different flavors displayed. Due to my budget restrictions, I chose only a single banana nut. I then walked across the street to a bench overlooking the river to enjoy my cone while watching huge cargo ships sail up and down the Savannah River. An elderly gentleman sat down beside me and proceeded to tell me that Savannah was the second largest container shipping port in the U.S., second only to Los Angeles. My trip was continuing to be an educational experience.

While walking on River Street, I happened across an inviting restaurant, The Shrimp Factory, located in a former cotton warehouse which dated back to 1826. I went in, took a look at their extensive menu, and quickly realized that, although their prices were reasonable, my $8-$10 daily budget wouldn't allow me to enjoy a lunch or dinner there. As I was about to leave, I had an out-of-the-box idea.

I asked to speak to the owner. I explained who I was, a little bit about my golfing tour of the U.S., and that I reported weekly on Real Golf Radio on stations in seventy markets across the U.S. I asked if she would be interested in me mentioning The Shrimp Factory on my Saturday segment. She said yes and asked what it would take. I said, "How about a complimentary dinner tonight?" She agreed. I thanked her, continued my stroll along River Street, and then walked back to my motel, all the while contemplating my upcoming complimentary dinner at The Shrimp Factory.

That night, my meal started with an amazing Caesar salad tossed at my table. This was a totally different experience for me, since the inexpensive salads I had been eating on my trip, although tasty and filling, were handed to me in plastic containers while dining at McDonald's, Wendy's, and/ or Burger King. My entrée was one of The Shrimp Factory's specialty dinners, Pepper Shrimp over Rice. I enjoyed it … actually, I devoured it … along with a glass of Chatham Artillery Punch, which was described as "a potent mixture guaranteed to cure all anxieties … for a while."

The earliest mention of the punch was in 1819 when it was considered a worthy refreshment for President James Monroe, who was in Savannah for the launching of the first steamship to cross the Atlantic. The president must have enjoyed a strong drink as its ingredients included wine, rum, gin, brandy, Benedictine, and rye whiskey. It was powerful, to say the least.

When I returned to my motel, I was full from a wonderful meal and quite happy about my decision to visit Savannah and the arrangements that had been made for me to play The Club at Savannah Harbor at the Westin Savannah Harbor Golf Resort and Spa. Named by *Condé Nast Traveler* in 2004 as one of the "Top 100 Golf Resorts in the World," it was the site of the popular two-man Champions Tour team event, The Liberty Mutual Insurance Legends of Golf.

The course, one of many courses Troon Golf manages around the U.S. and the world, was located between the banks of the Savannah and the Black Rivers in what was called the Georgia Low Country. It had straight, well-bunkered holes and both left and right dog legs, which, combined with its four water holes, made accurate shots of prime importance. It was a picturesque course as it wound gently through the tidal and wetlands areas, which gave me opportunities to view the area's abundant wildlife as well as take in outstanding views of historic Savannah. I finished my round with an 87. I felt this was respectable, considering I took double bogie sevens on the number one and two handicap holes. Once again, as at Brackenridge in San Antonio, I was thrilled to be able to play a course where so many golf greats had played.

When I left Savannah and began my drive to Augusta, my goal of visiting Augusta National once again began to overtake my consciousness. I was going see the most-revered course in the U.S. What came next was unexpected and disheartening. I drove up Washington Avenue and pulled into famed Magnolia

Lane, only be stopped by a very professional-looking guard who appeared quickly from his all-white guard shack.

I told him who I was and a little bit about my 50-week 50-state golf tour. I explained I was interested in driving up Magnolia Lane to the clubhouse. He gave me a stern look and said "that's not possible." He told me I could park across the street, come back, and walk up to a spot which he politely pointed out on the ground. He said there, and only there, could I take photos. He politely explained that under no circumstances could I proceed any further, as Augusta National was a private club for members only. I did just as he said. I parked my car across the street, walked back to the spot he had designated, and took photos down Magnolia Lane. I also took photos of the very, very uninspiring sign that read "Augusta National Golf Club, Members Only." The sign couldn't have been more than eighteen inches high and wide. It was very unobtrusive, considering the prestige of the Masters Tournament and Augusta National.

With my goal of seeing Augusta National still on my mind, I decided to drive the perimeter of the course to find a spot to take a few photos. Well, once again I was thwarted, as trees surrounded the course's entire perimeter—not just tiny trees, but trees maybe thirty to forty feet high that formed an impenetrable hedge. Although I was probably only a lob wedge shot from the course, photos of the course were impossible. I couldn't see so much as a blade of fairway grass through the trees.

I wasn't completely demoralized by my visit to Augusta, as I get did get to play Forest Hills, designed in 1926 by Donald Ross and redesigned in 2004 by Arnold Palmer. Golf history buffs will recognize the name Forest Hills as the course where Bobby Jones won the Southeastern Open, the first leg of his 1930 pre-Masters Grand Slam.

I learned that Forest Hills was perennially named the "Best Public Course in Augusta" by the readers of *Augusta Magazine*, and that it was the home course of the Augusta State men's and women's golf teams ... and good teams they were. The men's team had won the NCAA National Championship the two years prior to my visit to Augusta, and the women's team had excellent players as well.

I had the unexpected pleasure of playing with two members of the women's team. I was amazed at their talent, their graciousness, and their course knowledge. When I asked them about their backgrounds, sophomore Christine Duschek Hansen told me she was from Denmark. Freshman Stephanie Bennett indicated she was a local girl from Georgia. I asked Christine how she had come to play for the Augusta State Jaguars. What she told me surprised me to no end. She explained she had been recruited, and that most of the members of the Augusta State women's team had been recruited from Europe.

I was also taken aback upon learning that Stephanie was a redshirt freshman. Obviously I'd heard of redshirt freshman football, baseball, and basketball players—but frankly, I'd never heard about a female redshirt freshman golfer. This was another bit of knowledge I might never have learned if I had stayed in California and not left to pursue my goal of visiting and playing golf in every state.

I don't know how Christine and Stephanie have done since I played Forest Hills with them, but I do remember they were delightful young ladies, and that they usually outdrove me by a minimum of forty to fifty yards. In spite of my disappointment in not being able see Augusta National, they had made my day of golf at Forest Hills and my stay in Augusta most memorable.

South Carolina – "Great Golf and 60 Restaurants"

Besides golf, there are a number of benefits to driving to and through each state in the U.S. For me, seeing dramatic differences in geography was one of the major benefits. My visit to South Carolina definitely accentuated this benefit when I headed out of Augusta toward the golf mecca of Myrtle Beach on the Atlantic and then drove through the Blue Ridge Mountains.

Since I got a late start, I was a bit nervous as darkness began to fall on my way to The Reserve at Lake Keowee, the private, gated community forty-five minutes from Greenville where I was scheduled to play The Reserve's Jack Nicklaus Signature Course the following day. I was nervous because … to paraphrase words from the musical *The Music Man* …"I didn't know the territory."

Being lost in total darkness in the Blue Ridge Mountains was not my idea of a fun evening. Following the directions I had been given, and praying my portable GPS would follow those directions, I happily arrived safely at the Reserve's extremely comfortable Guest House. Since I was neither a paying guest, nor a prospective property or home buyer—just a vagabond golf writer pursuing a goal—I felt very honored to be a guest at The Reserve. It was a magnificent, 3,900-acre, peaceful, beautiful, and scenic planned and gated community.

That night, I dined in my room on fruit, cheese, and finger sandwiches which had been set out for me and the other late-arriving guests staying at the Guest House that night. I went off to bed thinking how fortunate I was to be invited to stay in such elegant surroundings and be given the opportunity the next day to play the exceptional Nicklaus course I had been reading about.

The next morning, after a hearty continental breakfast brought to my room from the main dining room in the Orchard House, the 20,000-square-foot clubhouse down the hill, I played golf with three Reserve members who were extremely gracious, to say the least. They told me all about The Reserve community, including the Marina, The Boardwalk, and the stores in the Village Marketplace. They helped me with my golf game by suggesting proper club selection for shots down the wide but hilly fairways. They also suggested distances for lay-up shots that would keep me short of ravines and pointed out the breaks on the manicured greens. They helped make my day on one of the few private courses I would play during my year on the road an experience I will long remember.

After finishing my round, I understood why Nicklaus said this about his course design, *"I really co-designed the course with Mother Nature—complementing the gorgeous natural features already here. It was my job to find the course hidden in the hills along the lake."* To my way of thinking, he definitely accomplished his desire. The course, and "the village by the water," blended together to make The Reserve stunningly beautiful and extremely welcoming.

That night, while preparing to dine alone as a guest in the Orchard House's upscale dining room, three member couples invited me to join them, which I did. Following a very pleasant evening of conversation and an exquisite dinner—which made me all but forget about the many $5.00 fast-food dinners I had been having since leaving home—I headed back up the hill to the Guest House to prepare for my upcoming four days in Greenville.

Not knowing what to expect, I was pleasantly surprised the next day when I drove into Greenville to find it to be a sophisticated city with a small-town atmosphere. It had museums, cultural activities, flower-laden parks, and a tree-lined main street, appropriately named Main Street. Thanks to Taryn Scher of TK Public Relations—who set up my Greenville accommodations, golf, and dining opportunities—

I ate at Soby's, High Cotton, and Nose Dive, three of the sixty restaurants located on six blocks of Main Street.

At Nose Dive, I enjoyed one of the house specialties, Maryland Crab Pretzel. When I saw it listed on the menu, I thought it sounded a bit far-fetched. But since it was a house specialty, and I had vowed to try all types of food on my trip, I ordered it. It had deviled crabmeat and melted white cheddar cheese on top of a German-style twisted pretzel. It was definitely different but definitely delicious. At High Cotton, the design of the restaurant and its upscale menu made me think I was in a trendy San Francisco or New York restaurant. At Soby's, I enjoyed their blend of contemporary cuisine infused with traditional southern ingredients. These three outstanding restaurants made me wish I could have stayed longer so I could have eaten at the other fifty-seven restaurants on Greenville's Main Street.

I played two courses in Greenville, Verdae Greens Golf Club, which for nine years had been home to the PGA Tour's Greater Greenville Classic, and Cross Winds, a Par 3 course which carried the distinction of being the only golf course in the world featuring a different hole by eighteen different world-class golf course designers.

Verdae Greens, located adjacent to the Embassy Suites Resort Hotel, was a challenging course carved into a lush Carolina Forest. It had gentle hills, mountain-like brooks that meandered through the course, nine dog-legs, and water on nine holes. My 89 from the 6,250 yard Whites, which carried a 134 Slope rating, was made with one birdie, three pars, ten bogies and four double bogies. I was glad I didn't have a bet going.

Playing Cross Winds was an exhilarating experience as I was playing a course designed by eighteen world-class golf course designers including Tom Fazio, Pete Dye, Rees Jones, Bob Cupp, Jay Haas and John LaFoy, a former President of the American Society of Golf Course Architects. I learned that John designed one hole and then called on seventeen of his friends and associates in the ASGCA to design a Par 3 hole for the course, which he and Sam Pate, the owner of the land, would develop. LaFoy and Pate put together a most unusual and unique course of 2,460 yards with holes ranging from eighty to one hundred and eighty yards with sixteen bunkers and no water hazards.

I had the distinct pleasure of playing the course while walking with John and Sam. What a thrill it was for me to speak with them and learn how they developed the course. I not only enjoyed great fun playing the course but was given an education about golf, golf course architects, and how courses are planned and built. Receiving firsthand knowledge from John LaFoy about golf course design was like taking a college course from a world renowned professor. John's resume included designing, renovating, or master planning more than 120 courses, including five years as a consultant at Augusta National Golf Club. He helped re-build numerous tees and bunkers at Augusta, re-built the famous 13th green, and illustrated Cliff Roberts' book about Augusta National.

While in Greenville, I made it a point to take time to tour the BMW manufacturing plant located in nearby Greer, midway between Greenville and Spartanburg. To say I was blown away by the facility would be an understatement of gigantic proportions. Never having been through an automobile manufacturing plant, I was totally amazed at the number of robots moving and welding parts, the safety precautions taken in the plant, the attention to detail of the inspectors along the assembly line, and the fact that all the BMWs at the plant were being made to custom orders placed by either an individual or by a dealer.

After my tour, I took an hour out to visit the Zentrum, BMWs on-site Visitors Center, which is the only BMW Visitors Center outside of Munich, Germany. There I saw vehicle exhibitions, engine cutaways, and very, very informative exhibits detailing the company's production milestones. Touring the plant and the Zentrum gave me hope that one day I could buy a BMW... and another reason to consider buying a Lotto ticket.

Off to "A Busy Week in Knoxville."

Tennessee – "A Busy Week in Knoxville"

When I received my itinerary from the Knoxville Tourism and Sports Authority, I was thoroughly impressed. The spiral-bound itinerary packet outlined five days of golf, tours, lunches, and dinners down to the minute with descriptions of each. I was definitely in for "A Busy Week in Knoxville."

Following my live, weekly Saturday morning report on Real Golf Radio about "Places to Play and Places to Stay" in South Carolina, I loaded my car and headed out toward Knoxville. After a quick, three-hour drive from Greenville through the Great Smoky Mountains, I checked in to the Hampton Inn and Suites in the Turkey Creek/Farragut area of Knoxville. It was a very convenient and comfortable hotel that had been arranged for me by the Knoxville Tourism and Sports Corporation. It would be my home away from home for the next five days.

When I got to my room, I set my suitcase on the folding suitcase rack, took out my bag of dirty clothes, and high-tailed it to the hotel's self-service laundry. To save a few washing machine quarters, I once again broke all the rules of washing clothes, and, except for my golf shirts and pants, combined my white and dark underwear, socks, and printed t-shirts in the same load. Saving a few washing machine quarters was always a consideration, as a savings of two or three dollars would buy me lunch. On my self-imposed $8-$10 a day food budget, that was important.

While my clothes were washing, I worked on future schedules, checked my email, and read the free daily newspaper I had glommed onto when checking out the breakfast area, which I subsequently frequented each morning for my complimentary continental breakfast. Oh how I loved those complimentary breakfasts.

My busy week started the next morning with the first of four straight days of golf, which in itself was going to be a real treat. I drove out to the Lambert Acres Golf Club, a 27-hole course in nearby Maryville. Opened in 1965, the course had an amazing history: not only had the Lambert family designed the course on their family land, but they had also physically shaped the land to build the course. Their work ethic was true American entrepreneurial spirit. I loved it.

The course was made up of three nines: Red, White and Orange. The Red and White nines each played to a little more than 3,200 yards from the Blues and just under 3,100 yards from the Whites. The Orange nine was a bit shorter at 3,047 from the Blues and 2,820 from the Whites. My 90 from the White and Orange combination was full of my usual mix of pars, bogies, double bogies, and—I hate to say—a couple of triples.

I played with Wes Cate, the Director of Advertising and Publications for the Knoxville Tourism and Sports Corporation. Wes was a very good golfer, having played for Austin Peay during his college days. My golf game was just so-so, but the day on the green, rolling hills of the former Lambert farm was great fun, as was the camaraderie with Wes.

The next day, Monday, March 12, Wes took time off from his office duties to host me at The Wee Course at Williams Creek, a beautifully unique par-three layout, and home of the downtown location of the First Tee of Knoxville. It was an amazingly challenging 3,200-yard Tom Fazio design with lots of elevation changes. Depending upon which tees were played, holes ranged from 64 yards to 245 yards along narrow fairways, with bunkers galore and trees a-plenty. As a Par-3 course, it was a real gem.

After golf, it was lunch at Tomato Head, located in the downtown Market Square District, which had a unique collection of restaurants, boutiques, galleries, antique stores, and nightclubs.

This fun eatery with the funky name was home to award-winning gourmet pizzas, salads, and sandwiches. I enjoyed my lunch, the first of the many hosted meals I would have in Knoxville.

Following lunch, it was off to a behind-the-scenes tour of the Tennessee Theater, a magnificently restored 1500-seat theater which was listed in the National Register of Historic Places and known fondly as "Knoxville's Grand Entertainment Palace." Next was a visit to the Women's Basketball Hall of Fame, which had an assortment of hands-on interactive experiences along with history and personalities of women's basketball—a must-visit place for fans of women's basketball. Then it was a visit to the Outdoor Knoxville Adventure Center, which was due to open the following month with a recreational information center and outdoor excursions and public programs.

Then, along with other members of the Tourism and Sports Corporation, I was off to the Ijams Nature Center, an interesting wildlife sanctuary and learning center with more than 275 acres of protected woodlands and meadows and over seven miles of nature trails.

It was now 5:30 and time for dinner at Calhoun's On the River. And dinner it was, a massive dinner of ribs, salad, and sides accompanied by a glass of wine. (I mention the wine because, unless I was being hosted, which was the case at Calhoun's, my budgetary requirements pretty much eliminated my adult beverage intake). Dining at Calhoun's, with a panoramic view of the Tennessee River, capped off a busy, educational, and enjoyable day.

My third day in Knoxville was a repeat of my first two days ... busy. It started with golf at Ruggles Ferry Golf Club in nearby Strawberry Plains in the scenic hills of East Tennessee, and then back to Knoxville for lunch at the Lakeside Tavern and a visit to the Farragut Folklife Museum—which, in addition to artifacts and photographs, housed the Admiral David Glasgow Farragut Collection honoring Admiral Farragut. It was Farragut, during the Civil War battle of Mobile Bay, who uttered the famous battle cry: "*Damn the torpedoes, full speed ahead.*"

The fourth golf course I played was River Island, known as East Tennessee's Premier Daily Fee Golf Club. I was told it was created to rival the country's most prestigious golf clubs and bring world-class, daily-fee golf to Tennessee. An Arthur Hills design set on over 175 acres, it had six holes located on an island and nine holes where water came into play. The course's website description told it all: "The course takes you over sweeping knolls, into lush valleys, below sharp bluffs and across a flowing river dotted with islands." I totally concurred, especially about the flowing river. I watched three of my tee shots take not-so-graceful belly-flop splashes into the river.

Following golf, there was a quick visit to the Mast General Store, one of a chain of eight stores located throughout the South, the first of which opened in North Carolina in 1883.

For a Californian used to visiting mall stores for my various needs, I learned what shopping in an old-time general store was all about. Carrying the flavor of the first Mast General Store, the Knoxville store had something for every shopper: comfortable footwear, traditional clothing, outdoor and travel items, and old-time mercantile items ranging from cookies and candy to wind chimes, housewares, and bird houses.

Charles Kuralt, who traveled the U.S. in an R.V. and had one of the original TV travel shows, once said this about The Mast Store: "All general stores are satisfying to visit, but one of them, the Mast Store, is a destination." Mast's founder, W.W. Mast, had a slogan I loved: "Quality Goods for the Living, Coffins and Caskets for the Dead." I suspect Mast was a good businessman in his day, and with that slogan, must have been quite a character.

I finished off my week with a tour of the University of Tennessee Sports Facility. I was walked through the state-of-the-art football locker room and onto UT's Neyland Stadium field. Knoxville has a population of a little over 102,000, yet during football season, the stadium's 100,000 seats are filled to capacity. This was my introduction to what SEC football was all about, and what an introduction it was.

I walked through the university's Thomas Boling Basketball Arena and stepped onto "The Summit," the basketball court named after Lady Vol basketball coach Pat Summit, who had led the Lady Vols to eight NCAA championships. I was also given a tour of the new golf facility, which was still being built and was to have three practice holes, five putting greens, a chipping area, and a driving range. (My alma mater, San Jose State in California, had a dusty field for its golf team to practice on). What a difference sixty years has made in the world of golf.

Not to be overlooked, other highlights during my visit to Knoxville included enjoying a quick visit to see and reminisce with old California friends, Bob and Donna Pabst, who lived near Knoxville; a "Blue Plate Special" lunch while watching and listening to a live radio show on radio station WDVX featuring local artists playing bluegrass; a fried chicken lunch with black eye peas, collard greens, and homemade corn bread at Chandlers Deli, where the South's first fast-food concept could well have been invented; and a prime rib dinner at Ye Old Steak House, a German-style restaurant where I was told that, on any given night, diners from as many as twenty states might be there.

Yes, it truly was "A Busy Week in Knoxville."

North Carolina – "Pinehurst Revisited"

As I left Tennessee headed for North Carolina, my thoughts went back to a visit I had made to Pinehurst some twenty-five years before. I remembered the wonderful little New England-style village, the church steeples, the flower boxes full of flowers with all the colors of the rainbow, and the many, many golf courses, especially Pinehurst 2, which I had played. I was looking forward to returning to the area known as "America's Home of Golf."

Prior to reaching Pinehurst, I stayed at my fifth Drury Inn and at a Fairfield Inn, both located north of Charlotte proper. Both had very comfortable accommodations, which was a great relief to me. While on the road, and not sure where I was going and what it would be like when I got there, it was always a relief to find pleasant and inviting accommodations, particularly places with complimentary breakfasts.

During my three days in Charlotte, I enjoyed a day of golf at The Golf Club at Ballanytyne, spent an afternoon basking in the sun watching kayakers tackle the rushing waters at the U.S. Olympic Kayak Team's man-made training site, and experienced one of the few frustrations I had on my trip: buying and trying to set up a new smart phone. After spending four hours trying to program the damn phone, I returned to the Verizon Phone Center where I had purchased it the previous day, canceled my new contract, and went on my way with another primitive flip phone. I was sure then, just as I am sure now, that I was born thirty years to soon to be able to understand and cope with the new computer chip technology.

My day of golf in Charlotte at the Golf Club at Ballantyne, an Audubon-certified public course, was spent playing under a bright and beautiful, robin's-egg-blue sky. The course, adjacent to the Ballantyne Hotel resort, was home to the highly rated Dana Rater Golf School. If I had had time after my round, I would have joined the novice and experienced golfers who were taking lessons. I would have enjoyed utilizing the private range, the chipping, pitching, and putting greens, bunkers, and the video technology in the indoor training facility. With my tee shots performing military golf ... left, right, left, right ... I could have used a tune-up lesson.

The course had gentle, sloping hills with numerous uphill and downhill lies, which, combined with its fast undulating greens, made for a challenging round. But with wide fairways easing its degree of difficulty, I found it to be a fair course. It was well laid out and in excellent condition for so early in the year. Its well-equipped pro shop, complimentary lockers, and well-trained and helpful staff were definite pluses in my book. With all the amenities available at the hotel, and the course only a lob wedge away, I think the Ballantyne Hotel resort might just work into my future vacation plans.

Following golf at the Golf Club of Ballantyne, I drove east for two hours to the Sandhills Region of North Carolina, which includes the Village of Pinehurst and the communities of Southern Pines and Aberdeen. *Golf Digest* has said that, with fifty courses within twenty miles of the village of Pinehurst, the Sandhills Region is the Number One area on the East Coast for best-quality golf courses.

During my three days there, I played two courses, Legacy and the Dormie Club. It was at Legacy that I had an unusual experience. I was paired with two brothers who drove down from Ohio year after year to play golf in the Pinehurst area. I introduced myself. "Hi, I'm Chuck Miller." The two of them looked at each other and started to laugh. That was a bit disconcerting until they told me they were laughing because their name was also Miller, Bill and Rich Miller.

We three Millers had a great day laughing, joking and talking about golf as we played Legacy, which was a Jack Nicklaus II design. It was an excellent test of golf skills with an abundance of trees, lakes, and fairway and greenside bunkers.

Early-blooming flowers in the numerous, well-situated flower beds, along with the Bermuda fairways—which I was told had just turned green in the past few days—added beauty to the course.

While playing, we were forced to stop under the eaves of a covered restroom to allow a thunderstorm to pass by. Lightning and thunder were normal for Bill and Rich, but not for me. Thunderstorms in my neck of the woods near San Diego were few and far between, maybe one every four or five years. I have to admit, I was both curious and cautious as the sky turned dark, drenching rain came down angrily, lightning flashes brightened the sky, and loud, bass-drum-like thunder followed. I was very concerned, particularly when I remembered "The Merry Mex" Lee Trevino had been hit by lightning while playing golf.

The next day, I played the Dormie Club, a new course that had been in business for only about a year but was getting a great deal of attention throughout the region. I was told that the PGA and R & A member who owned the land had hired the golf course architectural team of Bill Coore and Ben Crenshaw to design a course that would bring back the true feel of old-style courses. A couple of true golf aficionados I met felt they had done just that. They told me, "The Dormie Club is a golf course that would have made Old Tom Morris and his golfing cohorts proud." I understand the course has since gone private and numerous changes have been made since I played there. Even so, country club types accustomed to playing plush, manicured courses might find it a throw-back to the days of difficult layouts, relatively barren terrain, and spartan clubhouses.

When I played the Dormie Club, which had dirt cart paths; bunkers without rakes; sprinkler heads without yardage noted to the middle of the green; only red flags with no other flags indicating pin placements; and rough of natural grasses, native trees, and sandy and rocky areas, I felt I was playing a course more to the style of a few of the courses I had played in Scotland and Ireland. Playing the Dormie Club brought me back to the way golf was most likely played early in its history. It was at an enlightening experience, and one I thoroughly enjoyed.

The first two nights I was in Pinehurst, I was able to relax, plan my upcoming days on the road, and sleep like a baby in a spacious room at the Residence Inn. I was sorry I was only there for two nights and very disappointed when I checked into my next digs, a real pigsty of a room at a local motel that shall go unnamed. Fortunately, this was the first bad experience with accommodations I had encountered during my first two months on the road. Since I was getting comped, I realized "Beggars Can't Be Choosers," and I endured.

The next morning, I packed my car and began a five-hour drive to my next stop, The Inn at Parlor Hill in Orange, Virginia.

Virginia – "Three Presidents and Sam Snead"

After a quick and very pleasant five-hour drive through rural North Carolina and Virginia, I arrived in the small town of Orange, Virginia, home to the Inn on Parlor Hill, the first of seven B & Bs I would stay in during my lengthy golf odyssey. It was located just a short drive from Montpelier, the lifelong home of James Madison, the fourth President of the United States, father of the Constitution, and architect of the Bill of Rights. After settling in and checking for important emails about future accommodations and golf, I planned my next day's itinerary, which was to include a visit to Montpelier and a drive to Charlottesville.

When I toured Montpelier, which had been newly restored, I watched an excellent, short video presentation on James and Dolley Madison and Montpelier's history;

viewed some of the Madison's belongings and documents; and looked in at the Gilmore Cabin, where I got a glimpse of what it was like for emancipated slaves George and Polly Gilmore and their five children as they became citizens after the Civil War. I also took in views of the Blue Ridge Mountains from the Old Library where Madison did much of his thinking about the Constitution. It was an amazing feeling, realizing that I was in the office where Madison first envisioned the Constitution. Touring Montpelier was a walk through history and an awe-inspiring experience.

Following my tour of Montpelier, I drove for an hour on scenic back roads through rolling hills and farmland to Charlottesville to have lunch with Brigitte Belanger-Warner, Director of Sales and Marketing for the Charlottesville Albemarle Convention & Visitor's Bureau. She was a fountain of information about Charlottesville. It was a real pleasure for me to learn about the area from such a delightfully upbeat and knowledgeable person. After lunch, I window-shopped up and down Charlottesville's eight-city-block pedestrian mall, looking in on its more than one hundred shops selling fine antiques, shoes, books, regional handicrafts, clothing, etc. etc. etc. Although shopping of any type is something I try to avoid like the plague, I needed the exercise and enjoyed the crispness of the March weather. While walking and people-watching along the mall, I stumbled on and visited the original courthouse where Presidents Jefferson, Madison, and Monroe once practiced law. Another WOW moment.

My first night in town was spent at the Red Roof Inn directly across from the University of Virginia campus. Being hungry, as I was most the time, and realizing it was necessary to stay within my budget, I ventured into the local Jimmy John's sub shop located in the same building as the hotel. I was unfamiliar with Jimmy John's, but soon discovered that they were not only noted for excellent subs but for extremely fast service. In a matter of maybe a minute, two minutes at most, I gave my order, got to the register, and my sub was ready. Over the next few months, every chance I had at lunch or dinner, I ate at a Jimmy John's. Having spent over twenty years in the fast-food industry, I appreciated the quality of their subs, their reasonable prices, and their extremely fast service.

After a good night's sleep and a quick continental breakfast of hot tea and a cheese danish, I drove around town, all the while admiring the brick buildings and the grass lawns on the campus of the University of Virginia. I then headed to the Boar's Head Resort, a full service resort where I was going to stay one night and play golf on their Birdwood Course, an eighteen-hole championship course, ranked 4 1/2 stars by *Golf Digest*.

The Boar's Head, now the official hotel of the University of Virginia, was originally constructed from an 1834 waterwheel grist mill. In 1989, it was purchased by the University of Virginia Real Estate Foundation. Following an extensive $10 million renovation in 2000, the resort joined the Historic

Hotels of America, an elite program managed by the National Trust in recognition of historic integrity, architectural significance, and outstanding preservation efforts. My mother, who had a house full of antiques, would have loved the public rooms, as they were furnished almost entirely with vintage antiques. Again, I was very fortunate to have the opportunity to stay at another excellent resort.

The next morning, it was time to tee it up on The Boar's Head's scenic Birdwood course. Located on 500 acres of beautiful countryside with varied terrain and hundreds and hundreds of trees, it had narrow fairways, some pretty gnarly rough, and cart paths that ran up and down hills like you might find on a cross-country race course. Not long by modern standards, it was still quite challenging. It was walkable, but I learned most golfers who play it opt to take a cart. I did and was happy with the decision.

While in the Charlottesville area, I was given a private tour of nearby Monticello, the home of Thomas Jefferson, the author of the Declaration of Independence and third President of the United States. Now a World Heritage Site, Monticello had eleven rooms including the hall where Jefferson created a museum and greeted most of his visitors, a parlor with an elegant parquet floor, a dining room, a guest bedroom, and a sitting room. Although self-taught, Jefferson has been called an architectural genius for how he designed, constructed, and remodeled Monticello during a forty-year period beginning in 1768.

While touring Monticello, I was told that, to better understand life in the eighteenth century, I should eat at Michie Tavern, located next to Monticello. I did and thoroughly enjoyed a complete 18th century dining experience of delicious southern fare including fried chicken, stewed tomatoes, mashed potatoes, coleslaw, and biscuits and gravy, all served by servers dressed in period attire. It gave me a real flavor (no pun intended) of what it was like eating in a rustic tavern which accommodated travelers with food, drink, and lodging, and served as the social center of the community.

It was also suggested to me that I take time to visit some of the twenty-five nearby vineyards located on the Monticello Wine Trail. Although I didn't have time to visit them, nor the budget that might have been required to sip wine in their tasting rooms, I hope to get back to Charlottesville sometime in the future to spend time in the area self-proclaimed as "The "Birthplace of American Wine."

Another presidential home in the area that is not to be missed is Ash Lawn-Highland, home of our fifth President, James Monroe, the man who negotiated the Louisiana Purchase in 1803 and formed The Monroe Doctrine, the cornerstone of America's foreign policy, when he delivered his 1823 message to Congress.

I would have like to have stayed longer in the Charlottesville area as there was so much to see and do, so much history to absorb. However, my tight schedule had me heading to another Virginia historical area, Bath County, which since the 18th century had accommodated travelers from all over the world. I was about to enjoy one of the most interesting and lavish accommodations on my trip. I was going to stay at the world-famous, incredibly elegant and massive Homestead Hotel and Resort in Hot Springs, Virginia, a few hours west of Charlottesville. I was told that twenty-two Presidents, including George Washington, had stayed there. It was a massive hotel with 2,000 employees during its peak seasons. It was, and is, a landmark known the world over. At the time I visited, it was owned by the KSL resorts. Since then, it has become a member of the Omni Hotel chain.

The Homestead was one of the few places on my trip where I was not given complimentary accommodations. I paid a media rate of $75 a night to stay there. That said, the rack rate for my very, very, very spacious room was $750 a night with a Christmas season rate of $1,500 a night. The room across the hall had a plaque on the door which read: Governor's Suite. This was a unique experience for me, as this was the oldest, most elegant, and most expensive location that I had stayed in by far. I was a bit embarrassed when I rolled in my more-than-slightly weathered suitcase and my small, insulated bag which contained a new supply of Cheerios, milk, bananas, sugar, and teabags. Because I arrived late and couldn't afford to go downstairs to eat in the main dining room, I enjoyed a Cheerios and bananas dinner overlooking the stunning Homestead grounds.

The next morning, I had an experience I will never ever forget. I was invited to have breakfast with Don Ryder, Homestead's Director of Golf. I was more than a bit overwhelmed when I walked into the chandeliered main dining room with servers in starched white chef's coats manning a multitude of silver steam tables full of delectable breakfast items. I was greeted by Don, a very delightful and interesting man who had been a lifelong friend of golf legend Sam Snead and a pallbearer at Snead's funeral. I sat and listened for over two hours as he told stories of how he and Snead grew up together, how they fished and golfed together, and how Snead, at seventeen, started at the Homestead building hickory shafted clubs. I heard how one of the greatest golfers in history developed his golf game over the years, how he became the first Professional at the Homestead's Cascade course, and how he eventually became the Head Professional at the Homestead before moving on to The Greenbrier in nearby White Sulphur Springs, West Virginia. It was a fascinating morning.

Following breakfast, I grabbed my clubs and went off to play golf on The Old Course, one of Homestead's three courses, the other two being Cascades—which was built in 1923 and has been recognized as "The Number One Course in the State That You Can Play"—and the lower Cascades, a Robert Trent Jones course which opened in 1963. The first tee at the Old Course, which opened in 1892, has the distinction of being the oldest tee box in continuous use in the U.S. What a thrill it was to tee it up and hit from the tee box, which was not only the oldest but had seen Sam Snead hit from it so many times. I played with two of the course's maintenance workers, delightful young guys who hit the ball a ton. They had to stop after 15 holes to go and tend to their jobs keeping the course in the tip-top shape it was in. What a day ... what a memory.

After my golf game, I packed my belongings, gathered up my insulated bag filled with remnants from my Cheerios dinner, packed my underwear, which I had washed in the bathroom sink and hung out to dry the night before, and very reluctantly checked out of the hotel. I so wished I could have stayed longer, but knowing that neither my wallet nor my schedule would allow such a luxury, I drove three blocks to my next stop, the very comfortable Vine Cottage Inn, my second B & B in four days.

Staying at the Homestead with all its elegance, activities, impeccable service, shops, bars, and restaurants was like taking a cruise without ever having to go to sea. It was a fabulous experience. Staying at the Vine Cottage Inn, with its warm, friendly atmosphere and great breakfast, was also a true delight.

I felt blessed that I was able to spend a few days in Orange, Charlottesville, and Hot Springs, Virginia. But it was time to move on ... to West Virginia and golf at The Greenbrier.

West Virginia – "Tears at the Greenbrier"

uring the short, one-hour drive through rolling hills and valleys from Hot Springs to my next golfing stop—the world-famous Greenbrier Resort in White Sulphur Springs, West Virginia—I had time to reflect on several things. First, I was retracing the steps of Sam Snead, who had learned to play golf at the Homestead in Hot Springs and then had gone on to become the Head Professional at the Greenbrier. I realized how fortunate I was to be able to experience both these locations and these two historic hotels. Second, I was about to return to the Greenbrier, where I had been years before with my second wife, Dianne.

Dianne, who passed away from cancer thirteen years after we were married, was quite proud of her West Virginia heritage. She had been born and raised in Charleston, West Virginia's capital, where her father was the Chief Architect for Union Carbide. Tears welled up in my eyes as I thought how much she would have loved revisiting the Greenbrier. She had modeled there on numerous occasions prior to being selected to represent her home state as Mrs. West Virginia in the annual Mrs. America contest.

I also reflected that I was going to have to pay for accommodations for the next two nights, as I had no complimentary accommodations scheduled. Fortunately, I had done a preliminary review of motels in the area and had made reservations at the Super 8 in Lewisburg, just ten miles from White Sulphur Springs. It turned out the Super 8 had all that was necessary for my nomadic two day stay: a clean room, a comfortable bed, a desk to work on, and a complimentary continental breakfast.

Following a hot tea and oatmeal breakfast on my first full day in Lewisburg, I drove to the Greenbrier to play golf. The Old White, home to the PGA Greenbrier Classic, wasn't scheduled to open until the following week, so the Director of Golf arranged for me to play The Meadows, one of the Greenbrier's three immaculately maintained courses. (Now there are four). I took a cart, but the other two golfers I played with walked the course because of its level, receptive fairways. Although certainly not as difficult as the Old White, The Meadows was definitely challenging because of its large, back-to-front sloping greens which provided for some tricky putts. On one hole, I overcooked a fifteen-foot down-hill slider and had a forty-foot chip up a severe slope to get back to the green. So much for my putting skills.

Two other courses in White Sulphur Springs which I found noteworthy were the "down home" nine-hole Valley View Country Club, which I was told hosts many tour players when they are in town for the Greenbrier Classic, and Oakhurst Links, which was established in 1884 and is recognized by the USGA as the oldest organized golf club in the United States. Besides its age, what makes the nine hole, 2,235-yard Oakhurst Links so special is that it is played with replica nineteenth-century hickory shafted clubs and gutta-percha balls—and it is mowed by grazing sheep, just like the original Scottish courses. Although I didn't play the course, as it hadn't opened yet for the year, I was fortunate enough to meet the owners, who gave me a private tour through their on-site museum.

Oakhurst Links, which was purchased in late 2012 by Jim Justice, owner of the Greenbrier, had been the site of the Annual Hickory Club National Championships since 1998. Hopefully, the annual tournament will return there. I would love to have the opportunity to return White Sulphur Springs dressed in knickers, white shirt, and tie to play in the tournament.

Following my White Sulphur Springs experience, my next three days and two nights were spent in northern West Virginia at the Lakeview Golf Resort and Spa in Morgantown, the home of West Virginia University. On my 180-mile drive from Lewisburg to the resort, I got lost. My portable GPS took me to an out-of-the-way spot on the wrong side of Cheat Lake bordering the 500 acre setting for the resort. Luckily, this was the only time my GPS failed me during my entire fifty weeks on the road. Considering some of the back roads I traveled on, I was quite fortunate.

The Lakeview Resort had two championship courses: Lakeview, which played from 5,432 to 6,760 yards, and Mountainview, which played from 5,385 to 6,447 yards. Both were hilly, tree-lined courses. When I say hilly, I mean *hilly*, as flat lies were seldom seen. The Lakeview course had a lengthy Par 5, the 18th hole, a 602-yard monster from the Whites. To make the hole even more "fun," it had a slight left dogleg on its uphill, tree-lined fairway which led to an elevated green. It was a great finishing hole on a very interesting course. At one time, Sam Snead and Jack Nicklaus held the competitive course record of 67 on Lakeview, which over the years had been rated in the "Top 100 Public Courses in America."

The Mountainview course was more of a target course because of its narrow fairways and dramatic hillside location. Both courses had scenic views of Cheat Lake and the rolling hills of West Virginia.

I didn't take time to swim in the indoor pool or workout in the 40,000-square-foot Fitness Center, or enjoy a re-energizing treatment in the resort's Spa Roma—but, on my second night at the resort, I did go off my daily food budget to enjoy a succulent, baby back rib dinner and an ice-cold brew in the Legends Sports Bar. What a treat.

After playing four courses, visiting Oakhurst Links, and touring its small but extremely interesting golf museum; spending a couple of hours walking through the magnificent Greenbrier; and enjoying two relaxing days at the Lakeview Resort, I bid farewell to West Virginia and began my drive to visit and play courses in Maryland and Delaware.

Delaware/Maryland – "Bulle Rock"

W eek fourteen was quite an unusual week for me. I played golf in Maryland and Delaware while staying part of the week in Pennsylvania. For a native Californian who was accustomed to traveling hundreds of miles to venture out of the state, this was quite different, as the golf courses and my accommodations were all within forty-five miles of each other—even though they were in three different states.

My first stop was Havre de Grace, a historic city located at the mouth of the Susquehanna River at the head of Chesapeake Bay. I was there to play Bulle Rock, a Pete Dye design with natural grasses, gentle rolling fairways, creeks to avoid, long sloping greens and a few holes with Dye's famous railroad ties. I had been told about the course by Bruce and

Peggy McKinney, a couple I met and played with earlier in the year on the Dogwood course at the Grand Hotel Marriott Resort and Spa in Point Clear, Alabama.

Bruce and Peggy told me playing Bulle Rock, which was named after the first thoroughbred horse brought to the American colonies back in 1730, was a must if I was going to be in the area. Because of their enthusiasm for Bulle Rock, I made it a point to plan my route to be in the area and play the course. They were right when they said it was an excellent track. After playing it, I understood why it had been considered the #1 rated public course in Maryland since it opened in 1998; why it was highly ranked by all major golf publications; and why, from 2005-2009, the LPGA had chosen it to host the LPGA Championship.

If I had played from the tips, which played to nearly 7,400 yards and carried a 146 slope rating, Bulle Rock would have qualified as the toughest course of the 141 courses I played on my tour. Being of a semi-sound mind, I played it from the 6,000 yard Whites. Even from the Whites, it was a difficult course that required carefully executed shots, particularly to its well-guarded long sloping greens. (Carefully executed shots have never been my specialty).

The Par 5 11th hole, a real demon at 665 yards from the tips, was even longer than the 18th hole that I had played the previous week at the Lakeview Resort in Morgantown, West Virginia. Playing from the Whites, it was "only" 579 yards. After a drive, two fairway shots with my trusty 3-Hybrid, an eight iron hooked into a greenside bunker, a blast out of the sand onto the green with my sixty degree wedge, and two putts, I was annoyed but somewhat happy to have escaped with a double bogey.

While in Havre de Grace, I enjoyed being a tourist and visited the oldest continuously used lighthouse in the U.S., which was built in 1827. I walked the nearby boardwalk fronting Chesapeake Bay and watched locals build wooden boats at the Chesapeake Wooden Boat School. Since I barely know the difference between a hammer and screwdriver, watching the volunteer craftsmen teach students how to build wooden boats "the old-fashioned way" was a fascinating experience.

The second course I played was at the Deerfield Golf and Tennis Club in Newark, Delaware. Built in 1955 by the DuPont Corporation for its employees, it was now open to the public. A delightful Par 70 at 6,005 yards from the Whites and just over 6,300 yards from the tips, it was a hilly target course with numerous severely sloping fairways, left and right dog legs, and elevated greens. As the saying goes, it was "challenging but fair."

During my visit to Delaware and Maryland, I had excellent accommodations near the courses: the Courtyard by Marriott in Aberdeen, Maryland and the Fairville Inn B&B in Chadds Ford, Pennsylvania. The six-story Courtyard was larger than most Courtyards I had stayed in during my business career. In addition to 198 spacious rooms, it had a restaurant, bar, pool, and a workout room. Youth baseball teams from up and down the east coast headquartered there when they came to play weekend tournaments on the six baseball diamonds at the adjacent Cal Ripken Jr. Baseball Academy. My room overlooked the main diamond which, although smaller, was an authentic replica of Baltimore's Oriole Park at Camden Yards.

The Fairville Inn B&B in Chadds Ford was a relaxing inn with thirteen comfortable and well-appointed bedrooms situated in three buildings on five acres. It was an excellent place to relax, enjoy a delicious, home-cooked breakfast, work on my upcoming itineraries, and plan visits to nearby historic sites. One such site was the Brandywine Battlefield, where 26,000 soldiers fought the largest battle of the Revolutionary War. When I ventured out of my room and walked in the inn's lovely, serene, and colorful gardens, it was hard to imagine such a horrendous battle was fought only minutes away. It was a very humbling history lesson.

On Sunday, while at the Fairville Inn, I attended church a few miles away in one of the oldest churches in America, the Lower Brandywine Presbyterian Church, which was founded October 15, 1720—fifty-six years before the American Revolution. Meeting church parishioners who told me of the church's history was one of the many wonderful learning experiences I was fortunate to have while on my golf odyssey.

I next headed to New Jersey via one of the many East Coast turnpikes. This one led me through the outskirts of

Baltimore. Being a Californian unaccustomed to turnpikes and the method of toll collection, I cruised right through the "green light" lane, which I thought was a free lane. Ooooops! After driving unimpeded through the toll plaza, I realized I had just committed not only a mistake, but a possible crime. I didn't know quite what to do, so I kept driving, all the while watching to see if a state trooper was hurrying to greet me. Fortunately, nothing happened until a month later when I was forwarded a notice with a hefty fine attached for my transgression. I called the number on the ticket, pleaded my case, and was told to pay half the fine and my error would be forgiven. I was also given a stern reminder about being more aware when approaching toll plazas.

This was a learning experience, but nothing like the very uncomfortable one I would experience the next week in New Jersey.

New Jersey –
"Go Ahead, Call the Cops"

G olf was just one of the exciting things about traversing our great country, as I did for nearly a year. I had a multitude of different experiences. In addition to very enjoyable rounds of golf at the Atlantic City Country Club and the Seaview Bay Course, both just minutes from Atlantic City, my visit to New Jersey brought about two experiences I will long remember. One was walking on the wooden planks of the boardwalk at Atlantic City (which I understand has been rebuilt following its destruction by Hurricane Sandy). Having read about the famed boardwalk on numerous occasions, I had hoped that I would have the opportunity to walk on it someday; in fact, doing so was on my "bucket list."

But another New Jersey experience was, to paraphrase a golf term, "like going from the penthouse to the outhouse." This had nothing to do about making a great golf shot and then following it with a terrible one. It was about going from an almost-penthouse-type room at the Resorts Hotel and Casino, where I stayed for three nights, to a motel fifteen miles away that I now laughingly refer to as "The Dump." More later about "The Dump" experience.

Both the Atlantic City Country Club and the Seaview Bay Course were quite historic. Both had received considerable recognition and praise from golf industry magazines. In 2010, *Golf Magazine* named the Atlantic City Country Club the #1 Public Course in New Jersey. *Golf Magazine* also had, on numerous occasions, rated Seaview's Bay and Pine courses as Top 10 Best Daily Fee Courses in its America's Best category.

The Atlantic City Country Club, located just six miles West of Atlantic City, was founded in 1897 as a private club. In 1911, its first pro—John McDermott, at age 19—was the first American to win the U.S. Open. He won again in 1912 and still holds the record of being the tournament's youngest winner ever. Another bit of trivia about the Atlantic City Country Club: the course carries the distinction of being the birthplace of the term "birdie," which was first coined there in 1903.

The ACCC course played around and alongside bayside marshlands, and lived up to its reputation for having immaculate conditions and fast greens. Its fairways, in addition to being tree-lined with numerous bunkers, called for accurate shots to avoid the marshes and/or water which came into play on seven holes. The official scorecard labeled the course's tees with old and traditional names, rather than the various colors of the rainbow we see tees named on many of today's courses. The scorecard listed lengths as FRONT - 5,349 yards, MIDDLE 6,175 yards, and BACK 6,577 yards. I played the MIDDLE tees, which gave me all that I could handle.

Playing the ACCC was quite an experience, as it was a course where six USGA Championships had been held. Sam Snead had played it a number of times. Arnold Palmer played it when he was a relatively unknown Coast Guard enlisted man, and Bob Hope played it frequently when he was touring on the vaudeville circuit. (Am I showing my age?)

After my round of golf, while I was having a tall, cold one in the club's Tap Room Bar and Grill—which is lined with hundreds of memorable golf photos—I was told the club was the setting for the first discussions regarding developing a Seniors Tour. The first Seniors Tour event, which was won by Don January, was eventually held there in 1980.

The second historic course I played was the Stockton Seaside Resort Bay Course, which celebrated its 100th anniversary in 2014. For a number of years, it has been the site of the LPGA ShopRite Classic. It and its sister course, the Pines, where Sam Snead won the 1942 PGA Championship, the first of his seven majors, are the "pride and joy" of the hotel and golf club.

Both the Atlantic City Country Club and the Seaview Bay Course have views of the scenic high-rise skyline of Atlantic City, which includes the Resorts Hotel and Casino where I stayed the first three nights. Resorts was originally two hotels that had been built across the street from each other in 1868 and 1869, a few years before the Atlantic City boardwalk was built. It was the first major resort in Atlantic City. Over the years, the two hotels were combined into one supersize hotel. When I stayed there, it had just completed one of its numerous remodels and had enlarged its capacity to 1,300 rooms. While at the hotel, I ventured down to the casino—not to gamble, as my budget wouldn't allow for any losses, but to view the first slot machine ever used in Atlantic City when gaming was introduced to the city in 1978. I also walked the famed boardwalk and checked out a few of the other hotels, some of which have since gone bankrupt.

When I checked out of the Resorts, I needed a cheap place to hunker down for two nights, since I was going to be on my own dime before heading on to New York. I found a cheap motel in nearby Galloway, which unfortunately turned out to be a real dump. When I checked in on Friday night after golf, the rate was $33, and was going to be $66 on Saturday night. When my connections in New York didn't come through, I decided to stay in my shoddy room for five additional nights at the rousing rate of $18 a night.

When I told the motel manager I was planning on staying on for five nights, I was informed I would have to pay in advance for any additional nights. Evidently, a number of previous "guests" of the motel had skipped town without paying, after losing all their money at the various Atlantic City casinos. When I told the manager I would pay when I checked out, just as I usually did while on my tour, he became irate and shut off the electricity to my room. When I confronted him in the parking lot, he said he was going to call the police. I looked at him with as stern a facial expression as I could muster and said, "Go ahead. Call the cops." This stopped him in his tracks. Not knowing whether he was going back to his office for a gun or planned to come after me with a knife, I decided a better maneuver on my part was reconciliation. I gently said to him, "Let's talk about this." Once we both calmed down and I realized why he was so concerned, I relented and charged my next five nights.

"The Dump," which for obvious reasons shall remain nameless, certainly wasn't a motel I would suggest as a place to take the kids on vacation or spend the first night on a honeymoon. In all fairness, I have to say it was an okay place for "low-budget me" to stay. I was able to spend time planning my upcoming schedule, which would have me detour to Philadelphia to view the Liberty Bell and tour Independence Hall before crossing over the Hudson River on the George Washington Bridge on my way to Connecticut, my new destination and the next state on my tour.

Connecticut – "296 From the Tips"

After checking out of "The Dump" and a hectic, three-hour drive on New Jersey and New York freeways and toll roads, my stomach said it was time to eat. After crossing into Connecticut, I stopped in the charming town of Greenwich to indulge in a fast-food treat. I mention this only because it was such a pleasant moment of relaxation following contending with the hordes of speeding drivers who wove in and out of the lanes as if they were driving in the Indy 500. It was nice to get to peaceful Greenwich.

Following my quick lunch, I continued my drive to West Hartford, where I was to stay for four nights on my own dime. Once again, I had been unable to arrange comped accommodations. Although not a five-star hotel by any means, my digs at the Super 8 were clean and comfortable and definitely a nice upgrade after my nights at "The Dump."

I golfed twice in Connecticut, once at TPC River Highlands in Cromwell near Hartford and once at Lake of Isles near the Foxwood Resort and Casino in North Stonington. TPC River Highlands, the yearly site of the PGA Tour's Travelers Championship, was one of the few private courses I played during my tour. As I mentioned earlier, I wanted listeners to my weekly radio segments on *Real Golf Radio* to be able to play courses I mentioned.

When I teed it up on the Par 4 15th at River Highlands, it came to me what the golf term "Risk/Reward" really means. For PGA pros who played there yearly in the Travelers Championship, it had to be a tough decision. Only 296 yards from the tips, a hole of that length would normally be a piece of cake for tour pros, many of whom drive that far with a three wood. But the fifteenth hole was a true challenge, as water ran almost from tee to green on the left of the narrow fairway, and to the right of the fairway were numerous bunkers and trees, as well as a slight hill with gnarly grass. Coupled with these obstacles was a devilishly large green which sloped precariously toward the water's edge and was highly protected with multiple bunkers. I could only imagine the anxiety of considering an accurate tee shot, particularly when in contention on the final day of the tournament. It would definitely be a tough "Risk/Reward" decision.

I was told during the tournament that bogeys might be just as prevalent as birdies on the 15th hole. Looking at the water, the bunkers, the narrow fairway, and the sloping green, I was hopeful I could get a bogey. I played it safe … yeah, right … as if I could come within eighty yards of the green with a good drive. I hit my 3 Hybrid about 170 yards to the left side of the fairway, only a few feet from the water's edge. I then chunked a nine iron into the right hand bunker, blasted out to about fifteen feet from the pin, and sank a slightly downhill, curling putt that would have been in the water if it hadn't hit the hole. So much for "Risk/Reward."

(Side note: TPC River Highlands was the site of initial PGA Tour victories for two of my favorite golfers: fellow lefty Bubba Watson, who won in 2010, and Arkansas native Ken Duke, who was 44 at the time of his first victory in 2013).

While in Connecticut, I also played the Lake of Isles North course, one of the two courses in North Stonington adjacent to the Foxwood Resort and Casino, the largest casino operation in North America. I had a chance to try my luck there—"try" being the key word. Four losing five-dollar bets at the blackjack table, and my gambling for the night was over. I would have liked to have done more gambling, but I realized I had just blown two days of my food budget. The next hour plus was spent wandering throughout the six casinos and three hotels that made up the Foxwood Resort and Casino. With over 1,400 guestrooms and suites—plus restaurants, spas, retail shops, and the Fox Theater, where top name entertainers perform— it was quite a place.

The two Lake of the Isles golf courses, which are managed by Troon Golf, were both rated in the top seven in the state in 2011 and 2012. Due to my busy travel schedule, I was only able to play the North course. It was an excellent course with no parallel fairways, a multitude of greenside bunkers, and mostly elevated greens with steep side slopes. It had numerous holes with lengthy drives needed to clear marshes. One had a 220-yard carry over a lake. Playing the hole into a stiff, howling fifteen- to twenty-mile-per-hour wind was more than just a challenge. While I played from the Whites, the two young fellows I played with, who were big boomers off the tee, played from the tips. All three of us deposited our tee shots into the lake.

While in Connecticut, just as I tried to do in each state, I took time for some sightseeing. I visited Mystic Seaport, a recreated seafaring village. For someone born and raised in California who had very little knowledge of what a New England seafaring village really was like, visiting Mystic Seaport helped me understand something about America's 19th century maritime past. It was very enlightening.

I was able see historic vessels, some of which dated back to mid-1800's; to explore the preservation of the world's last wooden whaling ship, the Charles W. Morgan; view a fifty-foot scale model of the Mystic River area, which showed what it would have looked like from 1850 to the 1870s; inspect an interesting collection of figureheads and carvings from ships from the 1800s; and look at artifacts from the collection of Mystic Seaport paintings and photographs. Mystic Seaport was a great place to visit. It was very educational, with numerous activities for young and old alike.

Two of the six nights I was in Connecticut, I had complimentary accommodations at the Bellissimo Grande Hotel, a sophisticated yet casual hotel just three and half miles from Foxwoods. When I decided to visit Foxwoods, I, along with two other guests of the hotel, were driven back and forth to the casino in the hotel's private courtesy shuttle: a long, shiny, black limousine. When I got out of the limo at Foxwoods, the crowd in front of the casino turned to see who I was. I politely nodded hello, gave a Queen Elizabeth wave, and nonchalantly strolled into the casino. I felt like a rock star, even if my "Fifteen Minutes of Fame" lasted only twenty seconds.

From Connecticut, I was off to visit Rhode Island, the smallest of our 50 states in area, the eighth least-populated state, the second most densely-populated state (behind New jersey), and the state with the longest official name: "State of Rhode Island and Providence Plantations."

Rhode Island – "Shhh ... It's a Secret Course"

Rhode Island may be the smallest state in the Union, but it certainly has a great deal to offer both in golf and in other things to see and do. Most of my time was spent in the South County area, where I played four courses, all of which were privately owned and operated by local residents. That in itself was a big change from the California courses I had played over the years.

My first course was the 9-hole Par 35 Pinecrest Golf Club course in Richmond. Normally, nine hole courses are not my cup of tea. However, I had a most enjoyable day of golf playing Pinecrest because of its rolling fairways, excellent bentgrass greens, interesting course design, and the opportunity to play with local golfers as a substitute in their weekly golf league. League play was a new concept for me, as never in all of my previous golf—both in California and during my first three months on my tour—had I played in such a league. I had played on club teams in match play tournaments in California, but never as an individual player in a league. I loved the idea of the weekly competition and the camaraderie that was so much in evidence with all who were playing. We played each hole from two different tees on the 2,900 yard course, and although my 81 didn't win anything, I thoroughly enjoyed my day on a fun course with a new and terrific group of golfers.

Richmond Country Club, whose slogan was "a public course with a private feel," was the second course I played. Carved out of a pine forest, it was just over 6,200 yards from the Whites, had long Par 4's, a 230-yard Par 3, and eight doglegs that required well-placed tee shots. *Golf Digest*, which named it the "Number One Public Golf Course to Play in Rhode Island," was quoted as saying "its narrow fairways and towering pines give you the feeling of playing in the Carolinas." Having played in both North and South Carolina, I had to agree.

Meadow Brook, which was just in its third season when I played it, was the longest public course in Rhode Island. Shortly after it opened, it was voted the #2 Best Course in Rhode Island by *Golfweek*. Covering 225 acres, it had wide fairways, extremely large greens, and five sets of tees that ranged from 5,300 to nearly 7,500 yards. Before I played it, Meadow Brook was described to me as a "beautiful, picturesque, sculptured, and challenging course"—and it was. *New England Golf Monthly* voted Meadow Brook the #4 Top Course in New England and stated "Meadowbrook is sure to impress every golfer that graces its fairways and Rhode Island should be proud of it."

The fourth course I played was a "secret course" on private farmland. It was started a number of years previously, when a local resident built one hole on his property. Over the years, the family and close friends—who cut, mow, and maintain the course—expanded it to six holes, which ranged from 125 to 550 yards. Playing over small lakes, around tall bushes, and through narrow passages cut between trees, it was challenging and fun. The course reminded me somewhat of Scottish courses I had played because of its shaggy, shaggy bunkers; tall, gnarly rough; and its tiny, tiny greens. After each six holes, the course directions changed, with some holes hundreds of yards in the opposite direction from the original tees.

Playing this "secret course" was a wonderful and most unusual golfing experience, not only because of the uniqueness of the course, but also because, after every hole, the winner of the hole—or someone who birdied or made a sandy—was paid a dollar on the spot by each of his fellow competitors. Since the course was restricted to only family members and friends of the family, I felt very privileged to have been invited to play it.

While in Rhode Island, I stayed at the Surfside Motel in Charlestown and at the Stagecoach House Inn in the village of Wyoming. The Surfside Motel, a small, one-story motel, was a throw-back in size to motels of the fifties. Renovated prior to my stay, it provided a pleasant, quiet, and private retreat. I could understand why it was a favorite location for fisherman, kayakers, golfers, and those who enjoyed swimming in the nearby ocean. Since the Surfside was the closest motel to the Charlestown Beach, I drove there to view the beach. Because it was still early in the spring, and I was told the water was still quite cold, I opted not to add goosebumps to my body by taking a swim.

After four days at the Surfside, I drove north to stay at the Stagecoach House Inn. In the early 1800s, the Stagecoach House Inn had been a stagecoach stop between Providence, Rhode Island and New London, Connecticut. One of the busiest times for the Inn was during the Civil War, when General Walter Chapin and a number of his officers met there to develop war strategies while their soldiers trained in the nearby fields. Totally remodeled in 2001, I had a spacious room with a Jacuzzi tub, fireplace, and a view of the gently flowing Wood River, just a chip shot away. When not playing golf or working on my schedule, I ventured down to the river to talk with local fishermen, who told me about the river and the area. Throughout my year on the road, some of my most memorable experiences were the conversations I had with local residents like these fishermen.

When I left the village of Wyoming, I was headed for Salem, Massachusetts. However, even though my day was to be a long one, I scheduled a day of sightseeing in nearby Newport. I had been to Newport previously while on a cruise to Quebec City and Montreal, but had never had an opportunity to spend much time in one of the most heralded cities on the East Coast. I reached Newport just in time to take an hour-and-a-half, narrated tour of the city on the Viking Trolley. Following the tour, during which we passed some of the most luxurious mansions imaginable, I drove back to the Breakers Mansion to walk through Cornelius Vanderbilt II's incredible—and I mean incredible—seventy-room summer mansion. While standing in the two-and-a-half-story Great Hall, which was adorned with rare marble, alabaster and gilded wood, I tried to imagine the wealth of a man who could build such a summer home. I found it impossible to comprehend such wealth.

I continued my sightseeing with a visit to the International Tennis Hall of Fame, which honored the game's greatest champions and had a wide and diverse collection of memorabilia, art, fashion, trophies, and attire belonging to the game's biggest stars. Touring the Hall of Fame should be a must for tennis players young and old.

Next, I visited Trinity Episcopal Church, where George Washington was said to have worshipped. While I sat in one of the church's wooden pews, I gave thanks for my blessings and the opportunity to tour the U.S. I wrapped up my day in Newport with a shot of rum at the Coastal Extreme Brewing Company & Distillery, home to Newport Storm beer and Thomas Tew Rum. While sipping my rum, I was told the way it was made was almost identical to methods used during Colonial years, when Newport was the rum capital of the world, with twenty-two rum distilleries throughout the city. I realized I was in a truly historic city.

All in all, my day in Newport was just as I had hoped: interesting, educational, and relaxing. Unfortunately, it had to end, as I needed to get on the road to Massachusetts.

WEEK 18 – MAY 3

Massachusetts – "Vodka, Gin, Rum and Rye"

Seven nights on the road. Two hotels. Three B&Bs. Two rounds of golf. A walking tour of Salem, including a visit to the Witch History Museum and the Witch Dungeon Museum. Lunch and a tour of Woodman's in Essex, where deep-fried clams were first invented in 1916. A tour of the Cape Pond Ice Company, which had been supplying ice for Gloucester fishermen since 1848. A sipping tour of the Ryan and Wood distillery, where signature small batches of vodka, gin, rum and rye were being hand-crafted. A wonderful complimentary dinner at Rudders in Gloucester served by Francesca, a bubbly waitress with an effervescent smile. A Boston Celtics playoff game at the famed Boston Garden. Sound like a busy week? You're right on if you answered yes.

It was one of my busiest weeks on the road ... and I loved every minute.

My week in Massachusetts started when I arrived in Salem and checked into the Salem Inn B&B after a late afternoon, two-hour drive from Newport. The Inn, which is listed on the National Register of Historic Places, was actually three mid-1800 homes located conveniently in the heart of downtown Salem. After opening my suitcase, pulling out my toiletry items, and arranging clothes for the next day, I spent my first hour in Salem reading information about the city and organizing my next day's schedule. (I never totally unpacked or put away clothes in a chest of drawers during my entire year on the road. Working out of the suitcase was much handier and quicker).

The following morning, after a very nice all-included continental breakfast—I loved those all-included breakfasts, particularly where my accommodations were also complimentary—I walked throughout Salem's picturesque downtown visiting the museums and shops dealing with the Witch Trials of 1692. During the trials, hundreds of accused witches filled the local jails in Salem and the surrounding towns and villages. Some were fortunate to be acquitted, but some died in jail. Nineteen were hanged, and one old man was crushed to death. Standing in such a peaceful and charming city, it was hard to understand how this horrendous time in our history could have occurred.

From Salem, I drove northeast to Gloucester, America's oldest seaport, which is twenty minutes from Salem and forty-five minutes from Boston. I checked in to my hotel, the Cape Ann Marina Resort. My room in the year-round hotel featured windows and a balcony overlooking salt water marshes and the Annisquam River just inside Gloucester Harbor. I enjoyed watching small fishing vessels and sailboats glide effortlessly through the channel out to the Atlantic, a sometimes calm, sometimes treacherous ocean which, over the years, has taken the lives of more than 5,300 Gloucester mariners.

A sculpture at the Gloucester Harbor, just minutes from where I was staying, is a shrine dedicated to the memory of Gloucestermen lost at sea. Often called "The Man at the Wheel," it was made nationally famous in the MGM classic movie, *Captains Courageous*. A wall of remembrances with the names of the more than 5,300 sailors and fishermen lost at sea was added in 2000. While observing the sculpture and the names, I offered a prayer in remembrance. I wish I could have done more.

My two rounds of golf in the North of Boston area were totally different. One was at the nine- hole Cape Ann Golf Course in Essex, and one was at the eighteen-hole Hickory Hill Golf Course in Metheun. Cape Ann was a family owned and operated course which both locals and visitors have enjoyed playing since its inception in 1931. Formerly a dairy farm, it had three sets of tees which provided an opportunity for different length holes when playing 18 holes. Two of its holes, the 4th hole, a Par 4 dog leg left, sat on a hill and provided a panoramic view of the Essex River tidal marshes, the Essex salt marshes, and the backside of nearby Cranes Beach. It was quite a scenic view, particularly for someone from California who was used to seeing pines, eucalyptus, and palm trees.

The 7th hole, a 197-yard Par 3 from the Whites, was brutally challenging as it was only reachable by a long tee shot over the marsh. My double bogey five, brought about by my drive into the marsh, didn't turn me off, however, as I realized I had just played one of the "Top Hundred Holes on the North Shore" as recognized by the *North Shore Magazine*. Playing the Cape Ann Golf Course, although not as highly manicured as the ones we see tour pros play, was in its own way a most pleasurable experience.

Hickory Hill in Metheun was just a short jaunt from the Wyndam Boston Andover Hotel, a full-service hotel in the greater Merrimack Valley where one night's accommodations had been arranged for me. At Hickory Hill, I joined a group of thirty-five golfers who played together every Sunday. The front nine was perfect for my game as it had wide fairways which helped me locate my sometimes wild tee shots. The back nine was more difficult for me; it was tighter, with tree-lined fairways and well-placed hills and water hazards. Playing the course with thirty-five new friends in itself would have been enough to make my day of golf fun. But there was more.

When I answered yes when asked if I was going to golf in Vermont, one of the golfers told me about the Lake Morey

Resort in Fairlee where he and his buddies went twice a year for a golf tournament. He told me he would call the Assistant Pro and tell him about me. I was told to contact the Pro the next day. I did, and was offered complimentary golf and accommodations for later in the month. This was another example of the many fortuitous connections I made during the year.

My day at Hickory Hill had another unexpected plus. I was invited to help pass out promotional T-shirts at a Boston Celtics playoff game, which meant a free ticket to the game. This was quite a treat, since the last NBA game I had attended was in 1967 when I watched Rick Barry shoot his patented underhand free throws. Rick was a member of the San Francisco Warriors who played at the Cow Palace in South San Francisco. (A side note: during my years living in the San Francisco Bay Area, residents of South City, as it was known by Bay Area locals, resented the nationally known arena location referred to as being in San Francisco, when it was actually in South San Francisco).

With golf in Massachusetts completed, my radio segment written and ready for my live, weekly, two-minute-and-fifteen-second segment on *Real Golf Radio*, I actually had time to settle in for a relaxing few days of sightseeing in Newburyport, my next Massachusetts stop before heading for Maine. I found Newburyport, which played an important role in U.S. history as the eastern seacoast's first major commercial port, to be a delightful little city. It had a colorful and walkable downtown full of historic and well-maintained brick buildings. One of the buildings housed a most interesting museum, the Custom House Maritime Museum, which contained ship models, maritime art, and exhibits on shipbuilding and the history of the U.S. Coast Guard, which was founded in Newburyport.

My stay in Newburyport was very comfortable, as arrangements had been made for complimentary stays at two terrific B&Bs: the Compass Rose Inn, which had five, 500-square-foot suites, and the Essex Inn, which had seventeen well-appointed rooms and a history that dated back to 1890. Both offered outstanding 19th century ambience and 21st century state-of-the art comfort.

Following my three nights in Newburyport, I packed up and headed to Maine.

Maine –
"Two HUGE Moose"

Arranging for accommodations, both complimentary and non-complimentary, was a big task while I was on my tour. Fortunately, after working with state and local tourist offices, Convention and Visitors Bureaus, Chamber of Commerce organizations, and PR agencies, about eighty to ninety percent of all my accommodations during my fifty weeks on the road were complimentary. However, there were times when I was on my own dime for part or all of the time I was in a particular state. Such was the case in Maine.

During my drive from Newburyport, Massachusetts to Portland, Maine, I wasn't sure where I was going to stay my first night in Maine, as I didn't have an arranged accommodation. Because of my limited budget, Motel 6 locations were always my first choice, as they offered a bed, a desk, and a bathroom, and usually had the lowest price in town. I found one near the Marriott Sable Oaks in South Portland, where I was going to be staying the following few nights. Unfortunately, it was booked. I was able to find a relatively inexpensive room at the nearby Fireside Inn and Suites, which turned out to be an excellent choice.

After checking in, I opened my computer and finalized my two-minute-and-fifteen-second segment about Massachusetts for my upcoming Saturday morning segment, two days later, on *Real Golf Radio*. I had kidded *Real Golf Radio* co-hosts Bob Casper and Brian Taylor that even with my college journalism background, it took me at least four or five hours to be able to condense all my thoughts into the two minutes and fifteen seconds I was on-air talking about the courses, accommodations, and local places of interest I had experienced. Because I wanted to make sure I covered all the bases, I found it necessary to write, rewrite, rewrite, and rewrite again until I could get to the maximum 350- to 380-word script that I would be using.

Once I finished my script, I drove to McDonald's for a quick, fast-food dinner, returned to the motel, watched a little TV, started to read the local paper, and immediately fell asleep. The next morning, I woke up with the unread sports section nearly covering my face … and I was still dressed in my now-wrinkled pants and shirt. I realized my hectic schedule had finally caught up with me. After my usual morning shower, which I always needed to wake up, I dressed, took advantage of the motel's continental breakfast, and drove my car to the local South Portland Nissan dealer to have it serviced.

When it came time to pay the bill, I was told there was no charge. I questioned this and was told they had seen the sign on my car indicating I was raising awareness for Wounded Warrior Project while on the tour. They told me the free lube and oil change was their way of thanking me for my interest in helping wounded veterans. I thanked them profusely and explained that, although I wasn't a veteran, my son Mark had spent five years in the Marine Corps and that I, along with millions of other in the U.S. and around the world, appreciated what veterans of all wars and conflicts had done to keep the world safe. I explained that helping raise awareness for our wounded warriors was the least I could do.

I then drove to and checked into the Marriott Sable Oaks Hotel in South Portland. That night, knowing I was going to have complimentary dinners the next two nights at two of Portland's well-known restaurants—and realizing that I was in the lobster capital of the U.S.—I decided to abandon my meager daily food allowance. I did so by splurging on an absolutely fabulous dinner of lobster tail and claw meat in a butter sauce at the hotel's Fire and Water Restaurant. It was delicious!

On my golf trip, nothing was more convenient than being able to walk outside my accommodations and have the first tee on the course I was about to play only a short

Par 4 away. Such was the case the next morning when I played Sable Oaks, a tree-lined Par 70, 126 slope beauty. I recently learned that, in 2015, the course had been selected as the Best Course in Portland by readers of the *Portland Phoenix* newspaper.

The course, which wound its way through woods and across creeks and ponds, was all I could handle from the Green Tees–which, at 6,056 yards, were similar in length to the White tees I played on most courses. (Not quite sure why courses don't set specific tee colors). I think I played five or six different colored tees that were equivalent to White tees, the color most used to designate a course length of approximately 6,000 yards).

Having lived my entire life on the West Coast, I was somewhat familiar with Portland, Oregon, the city named after Portland, Maine. However, since I knew nothing about "the original Portland," I was delighted to have the opportunity to spend time in Maine's largest city during my week in Maine. After golf, I headed downtown.

I found that both Portland, Maine, and Portland, Oregon, had some similarities—particularly a wide variety of restaurants, from the very sophisticated to funky, artsy cafes. My dinners at two casual but upscale restaurants in downtown Portland—Zapoteca Restaurant and Tequileria, and 555— were excellent. At Zapoteca, which featured authentic Mexican recipes and 102 different brands of tequila, I was treated to a marvelous, mouth-watering rib-eye steak topped with salsa with guacamole on the side, and was given the opportunity to sample a few of their finer tequilas.

At 555, I had more of a New England dinner, an asparagus and potato soup, an entrée of herb-encrusted scallops, and a fluffy soufflé for dessert. Since my normal dinner meals on the road were pretty much limited to fast food from the likes of McDonald's, Burger King, Wendy's, and Subway, dining at Sable Oaks Fire and Water, Zapoteca, and 555 was quite a treat. I also enjoyed the opportunity to meet and talk with local residents, including two ladies I met at 555. One was the owner of a Portland and New York modeling agency, and one was a co-founder of a business consulting company. Having a fun evening talking with these two lovely locals about Portland and Maine was certainly an added bonus to my time in The Pine Tree State.

The Bethel Inn Resort in the tiny town of Bethel was my next stop after my visit to Portland. I took a small detour, however, as I had been invited to visit the town of Freeport and have lunch at Azure, a local favorite in Freeport Village. Azure, which specialized in seafood and Italian entrees, was located across the street from L. L. Bean's flagship store and a number of Freeport's more than 200 outlet stores. It was easy to understand why Azure was such a favorite of both locals and visitors alike after I enjoyed my lunch of New England clam chowder, Haddock fish and chips, and a dessert of a generous slice of vanilla bean cheesecake topped with wild Maine blueberry and strawberry coulis.

Wishing to digest my wonderful meal, I spent an hour walking around the L. L. Bean campus and its flagship store, a favorite stop for people from all over the world. There I came face to face with two HUGE moose locked in combat and what must be one of the largest boots in the world, a 16.5-foot-high, wooden, waterproof replica of L.L. Bean's famed signature rubber-bottom boot. Employees at the store told me the boot was the equivalent to a size 410.

Never having been close to a moose before, seeing these two HUGE animals with their antlers locked in mortal combat gave me quite a start. The moose, which stand inside the front window of the store, died in the Maine wilderness because their antlers were locked together and they couldn't separate from each other. They looked totally natural, thanks to taxidermists who spent hours upon hours putting them back together and preserving them.

Once back in my trusty 2004 Nissan Maxima, my next stop was the Bethel Inn Resort, situated on 202 acres in Maine's White Mountains. Built in 1913, it is known as Maine's premier four season resort. I was told that more than 35,000 guests visit the Inn yearly. Because it was between winter ski season and summer golf season, I was one of only a handful of guests at the Inn, although I did meet a number of local fellow golfers who were enjoying beers in the Inn's Millbrook Tavern following their golf round.

When I toured the Inn the next morning, and then played golf on the Inn's Jeff Cornish-designed course, I understood why *Golf Traveler Magazine* said the Bethel Inn "Stands as the shining example of New England splendor and charm … a true joy of a golf retreat." The Inn was delightful and the course, a true parkland course with tree-lined fairways, was a pleasure to play, although my sometimes-erratic tee shots often found me hoping to avoid the well-placed fairway bunkers as I pitched out between trees back to the fairways. With four sets of tees ranging from just under 5,300 yards to just over 6,600 yards, the course was one I felt would be enjoyable for golfers of all skill levels.

Sunday River was the third course I played. The Robert Trent Jones Jr. design had been named Maine's Number One course three years in a row by *Golfweek Magazine*. It was a definite test of golf. It had numerous hills with up and down elevation changes which allowed for scenic views of the spectacular mountain scenery. It also had a number of uphill target shots. Its rolling fairways, with few level lies and large, well-guarded greens with lots of movement, made for a very interesting round. The greens demanded approach shots that stayed below the hole if there was much chance of sinking even a short putt.

I played Sunday River with a local golfer who hit the ball a ton. Since he normally played the Blues, I did, also. At 6,500 yards—500 yards more than the Whites I normally played—I needed my best scrambling efforts to make the scarce number of pars that graced my scorecard at the end of my round.

I very much enjoyed my time in Maine, but after golf at Sunday River, it was time to drive to Sugar Hill, New Hampshire, where I was going to stay and play the oldest nine hole course in the state.

New Hampshire – "Sailing Through the Trees"

The Sunset Hill Golf Course I played in Sugar Hill was built in 1897. Located near the Vermont border in eastern New Hampshire, it held the distinction of being the oldest continually played, nine-hole course in New Hampshire. At only 2,002 yards, it had six Par 4's, the longest being 288 yards, and three Par 3's, the longest being 176 yards. To shoot par 33, I would have had to hit very accurate shots to extremely small, sloping greens from tees and fairways that were more like rough. The best I could manage was three pars in a bogey round of 42.

Even though I didn't score well, it was fun playing Sunset Hill. It was described this way on one of the course's colorful promo cards: "This historic-register gem plays virtually the same way it did more than 110 years ago, complete with authentic hazards like buried stone walls which render play a bit more strategic than it would initially appear."

The second course I played was the 100-year-old, 18-hole championship course at the Omni Mount Washington Resort in Bretton Woods. A number of years previously, I had driven by the course on a fall foliage tour where I viewed magnificent forests radiant with leaves of red, orange, and yellow hues. I wasn't able to see much of the course that day, however, as it was covered with a white blanket of newly fallen snow from a surprisingly early snowstorm. This time, its color was a manicured, beautiful green.

The course was designed in 1915 by legendary Scottish Architect Donald Ross and had been a favorite of East Coast golfers ever since. From 2009-2015, *Golfweek Magazine* named it "The Best Course You Can Play in New Hampshire." I was fortunate to have one of the young assistant pros assigned to play with me. Playing along with this young man, who could hit the ball a long, long way—and chip and putt with tour-like accuracy—made my day on the course a most enjoyable golf round.

Although I didn't play it, adjacent to the hotel was another course, the nine-hole Par 35 Mt. Pleasant course, which first opened in 1895. I was told it was a favorite of families who vacationed there in the summer months as it could be played at its championship length or as a six-hole or nine-hole course with junior tees and family-friendly pin placements.

Prior to my visit to New Hampshire, I was told there were two things I needed to make sure I visited: the Omni Mount Washington Resort Hotel and the Mount Washington Cog Railway. Following golf at Bretton Woods, I took a tour of the hotel, which was also adjacent to the course. It was built in 1902 by New Hampshire native Joseph Stickney, who made his fortune in the coal and railroad industries. Over the years, it had had a number of different owners. In the fall of 2009, it became a member of the chain of Omni Hotels and Resorts.

It was an extremely impressive hotel. Because of its wide, expansive rooms and verandas, its grand ballroom, and its overall elegance, it reminded me of the Del Coronado Hotel in my native San Diego area as well as The Homestead in Virginia, and The Greenbriar in West Virginia, two grand hotels I had visited a few months earlier.

In addition to being a playground over the years for the rich and famous, the hotel had historical significance as well. The Bretton Woods International Monetary Conference was held there in July 1944, during which the World Bank and the International Monetary Fund were established. It was also during this conference, which was attended by financiers from forty-four countries around the world, that the gold standard was set at $35 an ounce and the value of other countries' currency was tied to the U.S. dollar. For those families who still have gold purchased by relatives in 1944 at $35 an ounce, quite a substantial profit can be made, as gold at the time of this writing was well over $1,200 an ounce.

Happy as I was to be able to tour the Omni Mount Washington Resort Hotel, I was disappointed that I was unable to ride the Mount Washington Cog Railway. I had ridden two other cog railways—the Mt. Pilatus Cog Railway in Lucerne, Switzerland and the Pike's Peak Cog Railway in Colorado Springs, Colorado. I would have liked to have been able to compare the Mount Washington version to those others, particularly since the Mount Washington Cog Railway, built in 1869, was the first of its kind in the world.

The non-golf highlight of my week was a three-and-one-half-hour Bretton Woods Canopy Tour ride through the trees above the Bretton Woods ski slopes. It included eight zip line rides, which ranged in length from 180 to 830 feet, with speeds estimated at up to thirty miles per hour; three rappels to the ground from the tree platforms as high as sixty feet; and two sky bridge crossings from tree platform to tree platform. Since my rounds of golf usually include shots off trees that line the fairways, by taking the Canopy Tour, I figured I could get some idea what my golf balls saw when I sliced or hooked them into the trees. Little did I know they had such a scenic view.

My dining habits while in New Hampshire were over the top. I had big, delicious, home-cooked breakfasts at the Sunset Hill House in Sugar Hill and the Buttonwood Inn in North Conway, the two excellent B&Bs where I stayed. I had outstanding steak and rack of lamb dinners at the Sunset Hill House, which, besides being a B&B, was open to the public for dinner; a traditional Irish Stew dinner and a pint of Guinness at May Kelley's Irish pub in North Conway; and a marvelous, palate-pleasing entrée of sautéed sea scallops on a bed of white beans at the White Mountain Cider Company, also in North Conway. I have always been an "eat to live" type of guy, but after having such wonderfully delicious meals, I better understood those who are "live to eat" types.

Fun golf, relaxing days and nights at the Sunset Hill House and Buttonwood Inn B&Bs, excellent dining, and my first zip line experience added up to a great week in New Hampshire. However, as the week came to an end, it was time to motor on to state number twenty-one: Vermont, The Green Mountain State.

Vermont – "A Place to Enjoy INGs"

As I mentioned in my Week 18 Massachusetts chapter, when I played the Hickory Hill Golf Course in Metheun, a fellow player mentioned I should stay and play at the Lake Morey Resort in Fairlee when I was in Vermont. He was kind enough to call and introduce me to the Assistant Pro at that resort, who arranged for three nights' complimentary accommodations and golf. Of course, I was quite pleased with this opportunity, but I had no idea how pleasant my stay and golf would be. I was in for a real treat.

Established in 1905, the Lake Morey Resort had been owned and operated by the Avery family since 1972. General Manager Mark Avery and his brother Jeffrey, who was the golf course superintendent, were the third-generation of the

Avery family to own and manage the resort. Their stated goal—"To provide our guests with a pleasant, memorable visit achieved through superior guest service and genuine Vermont hospitality"—was right on as far as I was concerned, and would have been even if I had been a full-paying guest.

I was originally scheduled for only three days at the resort, but I found it such a wonderful place that I wanted to stay longer. Knowing my limited budget would not allow this, I once again thought out-of-the-box and asked to speak to General Manager Mark Avery about the possibility of a lengthier stay. I asked Mark if he would be interested in trading three additional nights for a 1,000 to 1,500-word article with photos in *Golf Vacations Magazine* about the resort and the golf course. He said that was a possibility, but he would have to check as to room availability. He got back to me and said that yes, he would be happy to do that—and in fact, he could keep me in the really nice room I was in, which overlooked 600-acre Lake Morey. The lake, and the scenic forest that came down to the water's edge, reminded me of lakes I had seen years before in Switzerland.

The Lake Morey golf course was no more than a Jason Day wedge shot directly across the street from the 132 nicely furnished guestrooms and suites at the resort. This made golfing very convenient. I was able hoist my clubs and walk to the Pro Shop, check in, and begin playing the resort's well-groomed Par 71 course, which had been the site of the Vermont Open for more than fifty years.

I could have walked the tree-lined fairways during my three rounds of golf, as the course had very few hills or elevation changes. Walking would have been an easy stroll. Since a cart was provided, I took the easy way out and rode. My two favorite holes, the uphill Par 5 542-yard 12th and the downhill 557-yard Par 5 13th would have been the only holes where I would have been huffing and puffing. My third favorite hole, the short 119-yard Par 3, was played over a deep creek bed to a small, well-guarded green that sloped backwards toward the creek. Just like the famous 17th hole at PGA Sawgrass, it was a much tougher hole than its yardage indicated.

The course and the resort are very popular with East Coasters. Each year, as many as 140 groups venture there from all over to stay and play. The week prior to my stay at the resort, 120 policemen and firemen came from Boston and Cape Cod to participate in their twice-a-year tournament at the resort.

In addition to my three rounds of golf, I had the opportunity to go out on the lake with Captain Ken, a local resident of more than fifty years who was thoroughly knowledgeable about the lake's history and its residents. Ken took me on an hour-long, leisurely ride around the perimeter of the lake in the resort's pontoon boat. I enjoyed it immensely as I learned a great deal about local life at the lake and the fact that, in the winter, when the lake was totally frozen over, it played host to ice fishermen, snowmobilers, and skaters who skated its four-and-one-half-mile Nordic ice-skating track. I also learned that as many as seventy-two teams came together annually to compete for the Golden Sap Bucket in the annual pond hockey tournament, held on the lake. Being a Southern California native, I'd love to go back in winter and experience not only that tournament but snowmobiling—and, if it wasn't really *too* cold, ice fishing.

If you noticed, my headline for this chapter reads "A Place to Enjoy INGs." Lake Morey resort was definitely a place that has plenty of "INGs" as in golfing, swimming, boating, kayaking, fishing, waterskiing, canoeing, tubing, hiking, exercising, relaxing, and dining. Although I wasn't able to take advantage of all of the "INGs" due to time constraints and the time of year, I certainly did enjoy golfing, boating, and dining.

The Lake Morey resort was the only place I stayed during my fifty weeks on the road where I was able to participate in American Plan accommodations on a complimentary basis. This was quite a benefit as, in addition to my room, it included a full buffet breakfast and dinner each night which included appetizers, salad, a choice of entrées, and a variety of tasty desserts. The first night I was there, I chose a grilled, herb-encrusted rib-eye steak along with carrot soup, a mixed green salad, mashed potatoes, a vegetable medley, and a delicious slice of "to difficult to resist" chocolate cake for dessert. I was truly blessed to be able to enjoy (particularly at no cost) such wonderful meals at a relaxing table looking out at serene Lake Morey, no more than fifteen to twenty feet away.

On an offbeat note, when I was in college at San Jose State in California, I became a member of the local chapter of Delta Upsilon Fraternity. One of my pledge requirements was to memorize the various provinces of our national fraternity. The First Province, which I still remember, was made up of chapters at Williams, Amherst, Wesleyan, Colby, Middlebury, Bowden, Brown, Tufts, Technology, and Dartmouth. I mention this only because I found out Dartmouth College was only a few miles from where I was staying. I decided a quick visit would be appropriate, so I drove to Hanover, New Hampshire, the lovely, picture-postcard, small New England town that is home to Dartmouth. Except for the cold winter weather, I would have loved living in Hanover and being a student at Dartmouth during my collegiate years.

Having some extra time after driving around downtown Hanover and the Dartmouth campus, I drove back the few miles into Vermont to visit nearby Quechee, Vermont, and the renowned Simon Pierce glassblowing and pottery store. (I still can't get over how close the New England states are to each other). Being a non-shopper on a limited budget, I didn't buy anything, but I did a lot of looking, which I have to admit was quite interesting and fun.

All in all, I had a marvelous time relaxing and playing golf at the Lake Morey Resort and taking quick side trips to visit Dartmouth and Quechee. And I should also mention, in addition to relaxing and golfing, my last day at the resort included a visit to the local coin laundry to do my weekly wash. After nearly three boring hours of watching my clothes tumble clockwise, then counter-clockwise, and then clockwise again in old, gray, industrial washing machines and dryers, I left with the realization that at least I would have clean clothes as I headed to New York, where I was going to visit and play golf in Rochester, the Finger Lakes Region, and Cooperstown.

New York – "Rochester and Cooperstown"

Although I had visited New York City on business and pleasure trips on a number of occasions, I really didn't know much about the state of New York. After a six-and-a-half-hour drive from Fairlee, Vermont, I arrived in Rochester, the birthplace of Robert Trent Jones, with my busy schedule in hand. It had been extremely well-organized for me by three different Convention and Visitors Bureaus. It had me driving nearly 600 miles; visiting eight different cities, towns, and villages; staying in two different hotels; an upscale golf resort, a motel overlooking the Susquehanna River, a night in a nineteenth-century B&B ... and playing four different golf courses.

It turned out that my week in New York, as anticipated, was not only extremely busy and very educational, it also included invitations to numerous breakfasts, lunches, and dinners as well as private tours of Rochester's first golf course, the Country Club of Rochester, built in 1895; and the Oak Hill Country Club, site of the 2013 PGA Championship (won by Jason Duffer). My Oak Hill tour was given by the on-site PGA official overseeing the sales and marketing of the upcoming tournament.

When I first reached Rochester, I did a quick drive through the city and then headed to my hotel, the Wood-cliff Hotel and Spa, nestled high on a hilltop overlooking the village of Victor, just twenty minutes from downtown Rochester. After checking in, a quick shower, and a speedy look at the nine-hole course located on the hotel property, I met my CVB contact for a business dinner at Dinosaur BBQ, a honky-tonk rib joint where I had a huge dinner of baby back ribs. Although I am comfortable in anything from jeans to a tux, the Dinosaur BBQ was definitely my kind of place: casual attire, great food, and a funky atmosphere.

The next morning, I was off to play Ravenwood Golf Course in Victor, recognized as one of the top public golf courses in the Northeast. In 2003, it was selected by *Golf Digest* as the "5th Best New Upscale Daily Fee Courses in the Country." It had wide open, gentle sloped fairways, good-sized greens, and a few holes where target golf shots were required.

My favorite hole would have been the Par-5 dogleg right 18th hole, which was protected by two bunkers guarding the uphill, elevated green. I say *would have been* because my playing partner from the VisitRochester Convention and Visitors Bureau and I drove by it as fast as our golf cart would take us. We were trying to get to the clubhouse before a fast-moving electrical storm caught us. We made it, but when I got back to the hotel less than twenty minutes later, the storm was intense. The lightning lit up the sky like a strobe light going off every few seconds, and the thunder, which shook the building, sounded like artillery shells exploding in my room. I was quite happy we had decided to quit golf before the storm arrived. I wouldn't have wanted to look like a scared, drowned rat when I joined a number of media people for dinner that night at 2 Vine, a very trendy, white-tablecloth restaurant in Rochester.

The next day, after breakfast at the hotel and tours of the Country Club of Rochester and Oak Hill Country Club, I wrapped up my two days in the Rochester area and drove a quick half hour to the Bristol Harbor Resort to play the resort's Robert Trent Jones 6,700-yard championship-length golf course. Again, realizing the shortness of my drives, and my reoccurring lack of a long iron game, I played from the Green Tees at a little over 5,700-yards. Bristol Harbor was a beautiful course to play. The front nine had wide fairways and stunning views of Canandaigua Lake, one of the eleven lakes in the glacier-carved valleys of the Finger Lakes Region. The back nine was tougher for me, as it had narrower fairways and more trees to steer clear of. Both nines had smooth greens and gentle, rolling landscapes. For someone used to playing courses with few, if any, flat lies, I didn't consider it to be a hilly course.

Following lunch in the resort's Adirondack-style dining room, complete with rustic furnishings, I was given a tour of the nearby Arbor Hill Grapery and Winery, which had products that have been featured on the Food Network and had won awards at New York City's Fancy Food Show. I sampled a number of their eighteen award-winning wines and some of their forty-five jams, jellies, sauces, mustards, vinegars, and salad dressings. After the tour and sampling, my CVB guides and I walked across the driveway to Arbor Hill's fun brew pub, Brew & Brats, which featured Bristol Springs crafted beer and specialty sausages. The beer was thirst-quenching and the sausages delicious. Then it was off to dinner at the Brown Hound Bistro, a charming little restaurant with only twenty seats in its 100-year-old house's dining room. If it wasn't for playing golf as many days as I had, gaining weight would have certainly been a bigger worry, considering the extensive wine and jelly and jam sampling at Arbor Hill, the sausages and beer at the Brats and Beer Pub, and Brown Hound Bistro's scrumptious dinner, which featured locally sourced, quality ingredients.

Feeling like a nomad but enjoying every minute, my next New York stop was the quaint town of Owego on the Susquehanna River. I headquartered there for two days and nights in a quiet room at the Treadway Inn overlooking the Susquehanna River, the nation's thirteenth largest river.

I learned about Tioga County while having lunch with a member of the Tioga County Tourism Board. We ate behind bars in an old jail cell at the Calaboose Grille, once the Tioga County Jail.

I then sauntered along the scenic walkway overlooking the Susquehanna, took a quick nap, and then headed to dinner at the Cellar Restaurant, which was owned by a couple with a "Never Give Up" attitude. Their riverfront restaurant had been flooded by disastrous Susquehanna River floods three times in less than three years. Rather than give up, they bought the building, moved up a floor, and once again became successful, fulfilling their slogan: "Passion for Food and Friends." I admired their perseverance and loved their food.

While staying at the Treadway Inn, I played The Links at Hiawatha Landing, a true links-style course just ten miles from Owego. Noted on its promotional pamphlet as "A Premier Course in the British Tradition," it reminded me of golf in Scotland and Ireland. Its windswept sand bunkers and ornamental grasses, combined with water that came into play on seven holes, made it quite a challenging course. But there was good news. There were no forced carries for me to hit over and no blind shots. Golf is a tough enough game, but long shots over ravines or water and hitting to spots when I can't see my target is something I try to avoid at all costs.

The Links at Hiawatha Landing was nominated in *Golf Digest* as "Best New Public Course" in 1996, and in 2002 and 2008, *Golfweek* ranked the course "3rd Best Public Course in New York State." With a slope rating of 129 and 6,200 yards from the tees, which was considerably more than most of the courses I had been playing that had a 118 to 121 slope, it was really, really challenging. Because of the water, the bunkers, and the hole distances, there really wasn't one shot on the course I considered a "just hit and not worry about it" shot. Even the two shortest par threes at 144 and 149-yards weren't easy ones because of well-placed greenside bunkers.

After playing The Links, I began a two-hour drive on country roads through rolling hills to Cooperstown, where I would stay one night at The White House B&B, a 19th century classic Greek revival home listed on the National Historic Registry, and one night at the Otesaga Resort Hotel, a truly magnificent resort built in the Federalist style. I was told The White House B&B was built by George Bowne, who reputedly amassed his fortune as a pirate in the waters off the southern coast of the United States. Both the White House B&B and The Otesaga Resort were conveniently located just minutes from Cooperstown's museums, shops, and restaurants and the world-famous Baseball Hall of Fame.

I found that a great way to get a real feel for Cooperstown was riding the Cooperstown Trolley, which cost a mere two dollars for an all-day pass. The village is small, so I had plenty of time to tour it before checking into the Otesaga Resort Hotel. While on the trolley, I passed by the Fenimore Art

Museum, the Farmers Museum, and Doubleday Field prior to getting off to visit the Baseball Hall of Fame.

I've been an avid baseball fan since age five, when I attended San Diego Padres games with my dad at Lane Field, the Padres' Pacific Coast League baseball diamond. Visiting the Baseball Hall of Fame was a wonderful experience. The hall, with its three floors of baseball history, should be on every baseball fan's "Must Visit" list. I particularly enjoyed taking a seat in the Grandstand Theater to watch the thirteen-minute digital multimedia presentation about baseball's highlights and viewing the Hall of Fame Plaque Gallery with its oak-lined walls filled with bronze busts of the game's greatest players, managers, umpires, and executives.

My final course outing was played in a drizzle at the Otesaga's Leather Stocking Golf Course, which is considered to be one of the East's most scenic and challenging resort golf courses. It had holes that climbed to elevated fairways and tees and had shots that needed to be carried over portions of Otsego Lake. It was a beauty of a course.

The two finishing holes, which in my estimation were the two toughest holes on the course, were my two favorites. The Par-3 17th hole could be played at up to 195 yards over water. The Par 5 505 yard 18th hole had an island tee and Lake Otsego running the entire length of the hole to the left of the fairway. Both holes were outstanding. On eighteen, playing it safe, I hit a drive which barely landed in the fairway. I then smacked two 3-hybrid shots that kept me out of the water and put me close to the green. I chipped on, made my putt, and walked away quite pleased with a score of 84.

Being more of a city boy, having grown up in the suburbs of San Diego and San Francisco, visiting the Rochester area and the rural towns and villages of the Finger Lakes Region gave me a new perspective as to the geographic nature and the diverse countryside of the state of New York. It was a most enlightening and educational week.

Next I was headed to Pennsylvania to learn about the Keystone State.

Pennsylvania – "Gettysburg and Flight 93"

During the years from 1776 to 2001, a great deal of change came about in the history of our country. While driving from Cooperstown, New York to and through Pennsylvania, I had a chance to reflect on four happenings in these states, three in Pennsylvania and one in New York.

In 1776, the framers of the Declaration of Independence met in Constitution Hall in Philadelphia. In 1863, the Battle of Gettysburg was fought, and President Lincoln gave what is considered one of the most famous speeches in all of history, the Gettysburg Address. In 2001, the world was rocked on 9/11 by the destruction of the World Trade Center's Twin Towers, the crash into the Pentagon, and the heroism of passengers on United Airlines Flight 93, which crashed in the hills of Pennsylvania not far from the Maryland and West Virginia borders. Three of these events took place in Pennsylvania.

During my week in The Keystone State, in addition to visits to Gettysburg and the crash site of United 93, I played three courses in the tranquil country settings of the Dutch Country Roads area of southeastern Pennsylvania. The courses, all described to me as "hidden gems," were Golden Oaks in Fleetwood, near Reading; Lykens Valley in Millersburg; and Mayapple in Carlisle.

The night before playing Golden Oaks, I stayed in an adjacent farmhouse that dated back to 1857. Being the only guest in the farmhouse was a bit strange, but not scary. Strange because I knew so little about farming, and to me, the year 1857 was so long ago. After checking in and enjoying a hearty bowl of Prime Rib Chili for dinner in the course's nearby clubhouse, I retired to my room. I worked on my upcoming schedule and my Week 22, New York report, which I would give live later in the week on *Real Golf Radio*. And then, a bit weary from my lengthy and eventful week in New York and my drive from Cooperstown, I hopped into bed and fell fast asleep.

It must've been a good sleep, because when I awoke, I was very refreshed—so much so that, after a quick breakfast (my usual cereal and fruit with a mug of hot, black tea) I went out and shot a four over par 76 with three birdies. In all truthfulness, I have to confess that I made my game a bit easier by moving up from the Middle Tees, which were just under 6,100 yards, to the 5,500-yard Senior Tees. I didn't realize it at the time, but I was applying "Tee It Forward," a new trend in golf that was being recommended by both the USGA and the PGA.

My next stop for golf was the Lykens Valley golf course, which is near Millersburg and just a short drive from Pennsylvania's capital city of Harrisburg. With numerous elevation changes, sharp dog legs, wooded fairways, and a stream that came into play on several holes, it was listed as moderately challenging. Given my 76 the previous day playing from 5,500 yards, I figured "what the hell"—I was going to "man up" and play from the 6,200 yard tips. I played to my 76 of the day all right, but that came after only 16 holes. I wound up with an 87. So much for "manning up."

My third course was the Par 71 Mayapple Golf Links, located three miles from downtown Carlisle. After my 87 at Lykens Valley, I decided to once again "tee it forward" and played from the Gold tees at 5,475 yards. Playing the relatively flat course, which had only a 108 slope, made my round easier. I shot 77, which included a nice run of seven pars in eight holes.

Following golf, I checked into the Comfort Suites in downtown Carlisle, an historic Preserve America town noted for its restored architecture and tree-lined streets. Self-proclaimed as "America's Automotive Home Town," Carlisle is the yearly home to ten car shows over a six-month period, which attract upwards of 500,000 buyers, sellers, traders, swappers, barterers, and bidders on everything from car parts to antique cars. Since my first car was a 1939 Ford coupe, I was disappointed that I missed by two days the Carlisle Ford Nationals, described as "the largest and most thrilling all-Ford event in the world." With over 2,800 Ford, Lincoln, and Mercury vehicles on display and/or for sale, I'm sure spending a day at the show would have been quite an interesting undertaking.

Before driving to Gettysburg the following morning, I visited and toured the U.S. Army Heritage and Education Center on the outskirts of Carlisle. It was an incredible experience viewing the history of the Army via documents, artifacts, and videos, and by walking the one-mile outdoor trail. The trail included full-scale reconstructions of a French and Indian War waystation; a Civil War encampment; a World War 1 trench system; a World War II company area; and an interpretation of the Vietnam helicopter assault at La Dang, the first major battle between regulars of the U.S. Army and the regulars of the North Vietnamese People's Army of Vietnam. In my mind, the Center definitely lived up to its slogan, "Telling the Army Story One Soldier at a Time."

When I arrived in Gettysburg in the early afternoon, I checked in to my motel, the Country Inn and Suites, where I was greeted with fresh cookies. Since I was scheduled to have dinner with my CVB contact, I ate only one ... well, would you believe two, maybe three? I was able to save room for a wonderful dinner at the Dobbin House Tavern. Built in 1776, the restaurant, which was in Gettysburg's oldest and most historic building, lived up to its reputation as the place for "Fine Dining in the Colonial Manner."

The city of Gettysburg and the battleground area were beginning to prepare for activities the following year to commemorate the 150th year anniversary of one of the fiercest battles of the Civil War. When talking with local residents and tourists, I began to realize the vastness of the battle. My Civil War knowledge—or I should say, lack of it—was showing. I had always been under the impression the Battle of Gettysburg took place on one day in one small area. I learned it was actually a three-day battle spread out over a number of miles.

My knowledge of the Battle of Gettysburg was greatly enhanced when I watched *A New Birth of Freedom*, an excellent film narrated by Morgan Freeman at Gettysburg's National Military Park Museum and Visitor's Center. It explained both the battle and Lincoln's Gettysburg Address. I followed viewing the film with a tour of the Museum and Visitor Center, which housed twelve museum galleries, a unique collection of Civil War artifacts, and a huge, 377-by-42-foot circular oil painting, the largest painting in the US. It was a monument to the soldiers, both Union and Confederate, who took part in Pickett's charge where Confederate General Robert E Lee lost more than 5,000 soldiers in one hour and the Battle of Gettysburg was over.

I also had the opportunity for a private battlefield tour with a licensed battlefield guide, including a few quiet minutes at the Soldiers National Cemetery, where 3,500 Union dead are buried. President Abraham Lincoln dedicated the cemetery on November 19, 1863 with his most famous speech, The Gettysburg Address, which contained only 272 words and took about two minutes to deliver.

Gettysburg is the most visited of all military parks in the United States. It has 6,000 acres of preserved, hallowed ground and more than 1,300 monuments and markers, which makes it one of the largest collections of outdoor sculptures in the world. Learning about the battle, seeing the excellent film about the battle, viewing the entire battlefield at the 3-D miniature diorama, and actually walking the steps where both Union and Confederate soldiers fought and died was truly humbling.

After four days and nights in Gettysburg, I checked out of the very comfortable and convenient Country Inn and Suites and began a day of driving that would take me to another very humbling location, the crash site of United Flight 93, where thirty-three passengers, a crew of seven, and four terrorist hijackers died. The plane, which reports indicate crashed upside down at 563 miles per hour, had been hijacked shortly after takeoff from Newark, New Jersey on a flight to San Francisco. A number of passengers called to loved ones to let them know they were on a hijacked plane. When they were told about the crashes at the World Trade

Center and the Pentagon, they realized what was happening. At that point, a number of brave souls decided to take matters into their own hands. They tried to retake the plane from the terrorists. Unfortunately, they weren't successful.

The memorial to the passengers and crew who died in this horrific plane crash included their names engraved on a white marble wall at the Memorial Plaza, which follows the flight path of the plane's crash. Although they were unsuccessful in their attempt to overtake the terrorists, I, along with millions of Americans, will always remember their unselfish efforts to save what most likely was the terrorist's next target, the U.S. Capitol or possibly the White House.

Being able to visit various battlefields at Gettysburg and the crash site of Flight 93 are experiences I will never forget. Hopefully, generations to come will not forget.

Indiana – "Touchdown Jesus"

When organizing my route from Pennsylvania to my next stop, Ft. Wayne, Indiana, I realized I would be near Canton, Ohio, home of the Pro Football Hall of Fame. I decided to stop in Canton in order to visit the Hall rather than drive directly to Fort Wayne. It was a good decision.

I spent three hours walking the Hall and learning about the nearly 300 members enshrined since its first class of seventeen members was enshrined in 1963.

Having been a football fan since the age of ten when my dad took me to a 49er game at Kezar Stadium in San Francisco, and having lived most of my life in the San Francisco and San Diego areas, I spent a significant amount of time reading about and viewing photos and busts of players from these areas. 49er quarterbacks Y. A. Tittle, Joe Montana, and Steve Young; Raider greats George Blanda, Gene Upshaw, and Fred Biletnikoff; and Charger superstars Dan Fouts and Lance Alworth were some of the players I paid particular attention to, as I had seen each of them play over the years. Walking through the Hall of Fame was truly a memorable experience, one I would recommend to every football fan, no matter which team is their favorite.

Accommodations in Ft. Wayne had been arranged for me at Hyatt Place, which was near Cherry Hill and Autumn Ridge, the two courses I was scheduled to play. I enjoyed both courses, as they had bentgrass tees, fairways, and greens, which were similar to the courses I was accustomed to playing in my native California. At Cherry Hill, which had a *Golf Digest* Four Star rating, I very much enjoyed playing the signature hole, the 125-yard Par 3 6th hole, which had an island green that reminded me of the 17th at TPC Sawgrass.

Autumn Ridge, the second course I played in Fort Wayne, had rolling terrain and spectacular holes with ominous lakes … seventeen of them, in fact. Although I did dump two shots into the seemingly ever-present water, I was pleased that I avoided most of the lakes. After my round, while sipping an ice-cold beer in the clubhouse, I was told that only two lake balls was quite an accomplishment for someone who had never played the course before. I walked away with a smile on my face.

My favorite hole at Autumn Ridge was the Par 4 13th hole, Autumn Ridge's signature hole, which had water all along the left side of the fairway. I liked it because it was well-designed, challenging and ... I never got close to the water and was able to par the hole.

During my stay in Fort Wayne, I took in a Class A minor-league baseball game between the Fort Wayne Tin Caps and the Lansing Lug Nuts (love those names) at Parkview Stadium, which has to be one of the finer minor-league stadiums in the country. I also enjoyed delicious ribs, baked beans, and creamy coleslaw along with hundreds of other rib fanciers at the 15th Annual Fort Wayne Rib Fest, held outdoors at Fort Wayne's Headquarters Park. It was quite a competitive atmosphere with trophies from all over the country for best ribs and/or sauces proudly displayed in each booth.

After Fort Wayne, I drove to South Bend to visit the campus of Notre Dame and play Notre Dame's Warren course, the home course of the University of Notre Dame Fighting Irish golf team. Designed by Bill Coore and Ben Crenshaw, with tees ranging from 5,300 to 7,000 yards, it was a real beauty. Since its opening in 2009, it had hosted USGA, NCAA, and Western Golf Association tournaments, including the 2010 Women's Amateur Public Links Championships. It was rated as the 6th Best Public Course in Indiana and the 12th best college course in America.

While on the seventh tee, I called my granddaughter, Katie, a graduate of University of Southern California, one of Notre Dame's arch rivals. We spoke for a few minutes and when she asked where I was, I told her I was playing golf on the Notre Dame campus with a father and son who were both graduates of Notre Dame. Her closing comments were a comical: "Have fun playing with the enemy."

Following golf, I returned to my hotel, the environmentally friendly Ivy Court Inn and Suites, where I caught up on emails in my spacious and very comfortable room directly across the street from the Notre Dame campus. Once caught up, I drove around the campus. I was able to gaze up at the university's famed Golden Dome and stop at the stunningly beautiful Basilica of Sacred Heart to say prayers for our wounded warriors. The Basilica, which was consecrated in 1888, houses relics of each of the twelve apostles as well as pieces of the manger at Bethlehem.

I also visited the Grotto of our Lady of Lourdes, a one-seventh size replica of the famed French shrine where the Virgin Mary appeared to St. Bernadette on eighteen occasions in 1858. Another highlight of my campus visit was my first glimpse of Touchdown Jesus. Jesus's likeness is depicted in a mosaic on the outside wall of the twelve-story library and can be seen from the football stadium. With his hands in the air, much like he is signaling a touchdown, Touchdown Jesus was quite an impressive sight. Since I had never before heard of Touchdown Jesus, my immediate thought was the name was a little sacrilegious for a good Catholic school like Notre Dame. Once I saw the mosaic, I realized why it had that moniker.

The next morning, after a hearty buffet breakfast at the Inn with members of the VisitFortWayne Convention and Visitors Bureau, I began a four and one-half hour drive to the Shanty Creek Resort in Bellaire, Michigan, where I would headquarter the next two nights. As I headed out of South Bend, I was disappointed my tight schedule hadn't allowed time to visit the Studebaker National Museum, which houses the largest collection of presidential carriages, including the one taken by President Lincoln on his fateful ride to Ford's theater. I was also unable to spend time at the South Bend Chocolate Company to see one of the largest collections of chocolate memorabilia in the world. I would have liked to have been able to sample some of their chocolates, which had been described to me as "the best chocolates ever."

WEEK 25 – JUNE 18

Michigan –
"700 Miles and Six Courses"

With top-flight golf resorts and over 800 public golf courses, deciding where to play in Michigan—which is self-proclaimed as "America's Summer Golf Capital"—was a daunting challenge. Having heard that *Golfweek Magazine* ranked Northern Michigan as #12 among the best places to play golf, not only in the U.S. but in the world, I decided that would be where I would play when my odyssey took me to Michigan. While researching the area, I hit the jackpot when I made contact with Kevin Frisch of Fusion Media Strategies. He made arrangements through his public relations company for me to stay at two wonderful resorts and play six outstanding courses … and he was my guide for the entire week.

I was very fortunate that Kevin was my guide. One evening after we stopped for a hamburger, fries, and a shake at one of his favorite '50s-style restaurants, we began driving to my next destination with Kevin leading the way. It was quiet when we started out, but not for long. Lightning lit up the pitch-black sky with continuous flashes of brilliance. Rain came down so hard, my windshield wipers struggled to keep ahead of the torrents. I couldn't see the road. If I hadn't been following Kevin, I would have had pulled off the road and started praying that no one would crash into me. I wasn't used to storms of this magnitude. It was surreal. I was frightened for more than a half hour as the storm continued to pound us, but I kept going, mostly out of fear that if I lost sight of Kevin, I would be in a heap of trouble.

The first course Kevin arranged for me was Kingsley Club, a private course just fifteen minutes from the popular vacation destination of Traverse City. It was unusual in that it had the feel of a links course, yet it was located in and through a lovely forest setting. In 2006, Owner/Publisher Jack Purcell of *Links Magazine* described the Kingsley Club, which opened in 2001, as "the closest thing I've experienced in America to an inland Scottish or Irish course."

I played from the "regular tees" at 6,300 yards, which gave me all I could handle plus some.

Because of its unique landforms, its firm, fast fairways and greens, and wind that was blowing briskly, each shot took careful consideration. It was a course that had various options on every shot. "Below the hole" was imperative as the bentgrass greens were not only slick and fast but had severe slopes and undulations.

The second course I played was Cedar River Golf Club, one of four courses at the Shanty Creek Resort in Bellaire, where I stayed. Shanty Creek, a four-season resort with seventy-two holes of golf, fifty-three downhill ski slopes, and thirty kilometers of cross-country trails, was located on 4,500 acres just thirty miles northeast of Traverse City. It boasted three distinct villages, award-winning dining, live entertainment, and a full-service conference/banquet center. It was a wonderful place to stay.

The Tom Weiskopf-designed course had rolling hills, peaceful waters, stunning views, and five sets of tees that stretched the course from 5,300 yards to just under 7,000 yards. Named one of America's Top 100 Resort Courses by *Golfweek* and one of *Golf Magazine's* "Top Ten in the U. S. You Can Play," the course was in immaculate condition. Playing through the forest on a course with no parallel fairways, dramatic elevation changes, and well-designed holes around lakes was a real pleasure.

My third course was Bay Harbor Golf Club in Petoskey, one of eleven courses in Northern Michigan in the Boyne Group of Resorts and Courses. It was located just a few miles from the Inn at Bay Harbor, a Renaissance Golf Resort with 134 luxurious hotel rooms and suites. Bay Harbor, an Arthur Hills design, had three distinctly different championship length nines: The Links, which looked and played like an Irish seaside course; The Preserve, an inland nine with hardwoods, lush grasses, wildflowers, and wetlands; and The Quarry, played in, around, and through an abandoned shale quarry with forty-foot gorges, steep cliffs, natural ponds, and a gentle waterfall. While playing the Links and Quarry nines, I had trouble concentrating on my golf game because of the gorgeous views of Lake Michigan's rocky coastline and various colors.

In its inaugural season in 1998, Bay Harbor was ranked eighth on Golf Digest's list of "Best Courses You Can Play." It continues to receive accolades because of outstanding course conditions, superb scenic vistas, and challenging holes.

The fourth and fifth courses I played were located at the Treetops Resort and Spa, which is in Gaylord, approximately sixty miles from Traverse City. The year-round resort had eighty-one holes of championship golf on five distinct courses, including "Masterpiece" by Robert Trent Jones, Sr.; "Premier" by Tom Fazio; and three courses by resort owner and noted golf course architect Rick Smith. For a number of years, Smith's nine-hole Par 3 Threetops has been consistently ranked the #1 Par 3 course in America. For a number of years, it also was the site of ESPN's Par-3 Shootout. Lee Trevino won $1,000,000 in 2001 during the Shootout by making a hole-in-one on Threetops' severely sloped, back-to-front 150-yard 7th hole.

The "Premier" course, Fazio's only course in Michigan, had the familiar traits of a Fazio course: tee shots to sloping fairways and fairway shots to numerous large, elevated, undulating, and fast greens. It played from 5,039 yards to 6,832 yards with no parallel fairways. My favorite hole was the Par 3 11th hole, the only hole on the course where water came into play.

My final day in Michigan, I drove an hour south from Treetops to play the Forest Dunes Golf Club course in Roscommon. Forest Dunes was a Par 72 gem designed by Tom Weiskopf that has drawn comparisons to two of America's top courses, Pine Valley and Augusta National. The course, which was surrounded by 400,000 acres of the Huron National Forest, had a very natural setting. "The Forest Nine" was tree-lined and the back nine, "The Dunes Nine," was links-style with native wasteland, wild grasses, and over eighteen acres of natural dunes from which it took its name.

Two rather unique aspects of Forest Dunes were the 3,084-yard tees, perfect for juniors, and a 110 yard Par 3 19th hole at the end of regulation, which had a bunker in the middle of the green. Not to be confused with 19th holes where matches are relived and adult beverages are consumed, Forest Dunes' 19th hole was there to give golfers an extra hole to decide even matches.

After playing both traditional and links-style courses designed by Arnold Palmer, Arthur Hills, Tom Weiskopf, Rick Smith, Tom Fazio, and Robert Trent Jones, Sr., I understood why the Northern Michigan area rated so high. Set in both flat and hilly terrains, in lush forests, sand-covered dunes, and scenic lakeside settings, the courses offered me a variety of challenging golf opportunities.

Even though it was an extremely busy week, during which I drove over 700 miles and experienced a lightning and thunder storm that almost stopped me in my tracks, I was thrilled I had the opportunity to stay and play in Northern Michigan. The resorts, the courses, and the scenic beauty of the area were all outstanding.

Idaho –
"Family and the 4th of July"

After a very busy week in Northern Michigan, I drove to Ann Arbor to visit friends for three days. On the fourth day, I was off to Detroit for one night before flying to Spokane, Washington and driving to Twin Lakes Village, near Coeur d'Alene, Idaho for a reunion with my family and the family of my brother and sister-in-law, Chuck and Ann Stone.

Twelve straight days of relaxing with family and friends, with no long-distance driving, no early morning tee times, and very few phone calls or emails, made for a most delightful and pleasurable time. Quite a difference from the previous nearly six months, when I had been on the road with its daily grind of twelve- to fifteen-hour days driving, golfing, and organizing. Okay ... okay, golfing really wasn't that difficult to do and enjoy.

In addition to the wonderful time with fifteen members of our families, I did take time out to play two courses, Twin Lakes Village and nearby Circling Raven, which is located in Worley about forty-five minutes from both Twin Lakes and Spokane.

Playing Twin Lakes was a wonderful and competitive round of golf because it was in a family reunion scramble pitting the Miller side of the family against the Stone side of the family. Unfortunately, the Miller family team was soundly defeated by the Stone team. (This past year, the tournament results were the same). But we're going to fix that! The Miller family team is now buying lotto tickets so that we can hire some of the best PGA pros and adopt them into our family. Then, with more skill on our team, we'll whip the Stone team's derrière.

The Twin Lakes course was a very friendly and family-oriented course with tees ranging from 2,800 to 6,300 yards. Except for the Par 4 3rd hole with its highly elevated tee, the course was easy to walk, as it was delightfully flat as a pancake. However, because of its narrow, tree-lined fairways, water on twelve holes, and small greens, it was a tougher test than its yardage and topography would suggest.

If and when you ever play Twin Lakes, make sure to take some quarters for the small vending machine on the Par 3 15th hole, where you can buy feed for the huge—and

I mean *huge*—rainbow trout in the hole's pond. When you throw the pellet feed into the water, you'll see an amazing feeding frenzy. Never having cruised the Amazon or seen piranha devour anything thrown at them, I'm not sure this trout frenzy would compare, but it was quite a sight.

Circling Raven, the second course I played, was a links-style course owned and operated by the Coeur d'Alene Indian tribe. Situated on 620 acres of lush forests, grassy meadows, and carefully preserved wetlands, it was designed by golf course architect Gene Bates, who blended the course with nature rather than competing against it.

In 2005, Circling Raven was voted as a Top 10 Best New Upscale Course by *Golf Digest,* and since then it has received numerous awards including recognition by *Golf Magazine* in 2010-2011 as one of America's Top Courses You Can Play. At 6,180 yards with a 131 slope from the Whites, it was a demanding course with wide, sloping fairways and multiple, well-placed fairway and greenside bunkers. My favorite hole was the downhill 205 yard Par 3 thirteenth which required a tee shot of 180 yards to clear the native grasses to get to a back-to-front sloping green. I made it over and got high-fives from my fellow golfers.

Although I didn't play it this time, while in Idaho, the Coeur d'Alene Resort Course, home of the world's only moveable-island green, should be a "must play" course for every golfer. Hitting to a green totally surrounded by water, which can be moved from 150 to 195 yards across a portion of Lake Coeur d'Alene, is a real thrill. If you hit the green—or don't hit it in two tries—you board a boat which takes you to the green. If by luck or skill you have an ace, birdie, or par on the hole, you are awarded a Certificate of Achievement recognizing the accomplishment.

One day while at Twin Lakes, a number of us drove to Spokane to attend the 23rd Annual Hoop Fest, the largest "Three on Three" basketball tournament on earth. Over 28,000 players on more than 7,000 teams played the two-day event on 420 half-courts scattered throughout Spokane's downtown. It was an amazing, city-backed event. I, and the rest of our clan, went there to root for my brother-in-law's grandson, Nick, whose team had made it to the finals in their division.

Besides the family camaraderie, the barbecues, and the ice cold Kokanee and Rolling Rock beers we all enjoyed, a highlight for all of us was the village's Fourth of July activities. The residents of the village celebrated with a parade of golf carts decorated with red, white, and blue flags waving in the breeze and an annual and very moving Fourth of July flag-raising ceremony. The ceremony included a flyover of vintage airplanes, musket firings, patriotic songs, the Pledge of Allegiance recited by a four-year-old, the singing of the Star Spangled Banner, and the playing of taps honoring those who died in the service of our country. I was asked to speak briefly about the Wounded Warrior Project and how it helped Iraq and Afghanistan wounded veterans. I felt very honored. Enjoying the Fourth of July with family and friends as we gave tribute to the founding of our nation was an emotional experience.

Spending time with the Miller and Stone families was terrific. Chuck Stone and I had known each other since 1957, when he attended Santa Clara University and I attended San Jose State, both located in the San Jose, California area. We met because my first wife, Carolyn, and Chuck's wife, Ann. were sisters. We have been blessed that we and our children have stayed close all these years. Now our grandchildren are also close. Every time we get together and I see the love between our families, it points out to me the importance of family in our society.

Following our reunion, I was driven back to Spokane, where I hopped a plane to Detroit and drove to Cleveland, Ohio, my next stop in my next state.

Ohio – "Rock & Roll and Baseball"

The trip from the Detroit airport to Cleveland was a short drive. Never having been to Cleveland, I was looking forward to my first visit, although I must admit the only things I had heard about the downtown area were … well, let's say … not exactly complimentary. However, the Positively Cleveland Convention and Visitors Bureau had an interesting two-day itinerary for me, so I approached the city and the area with an open mind.

My first day in downtown Cleveland dramatically dispelled all the negative things I had heard. The area was vibrant, clean, fun, and tourist-friendly. Over two billion dollars had been spent on tourism projects including the new Horseshoe Casino Cleveland, the Greater Cleveland

Aquarium, the Cleveland Medical Mart, and the Convention Center. I was told the major revitalization program was bringing both businesses and tourists back downtown. I looked forward to enjoying my short time in Cleveland.

My accommodations had been arranged at the Courtyard Cleveland South in Independence, about a twenty-minute drive from both downtown Cleveland and the Sleepy Hollow Golf Club, where I was scheduled to play. After checking in, I headed downtown to the first stop on my itinerary, the Rock and Roll Hall of Fame and Museum.

Built on the shores of Lake Erie, the museum opened in 1995 after twelve years in the making. It was an impressive concrete and glass, seven-story structure designed by world-renown architect I. M. Pei. During his six decades of architectural work, in addition to the Rock and Roll Hall of Fame and Museum, Pei had designed some of the most recognizable buildings in the world including the Century Towers in Los Angeles, the John F. Kennedy Library in Boston, and the Louvre Pyramid in Paris. The Hall's pyramid-like shape, designed to reflect a guitar shooting up to the sky, was stunning, but the real attraction for me was the Hall's five floors of exhibits and memorabilia.

During the four hours I roamed the Hall, I watched videos, checked out artifacts and memorabilia, sang along with the Beatles and Elvis, rocked with Jimi Hendrix and Janis Joplin, and visited a major exhibition dedicated to the Grateful Dead. My time spent at the Hall of Fame gave me a much greater insight into many of the rock stars I had heard and seen over the years. It was a terrific four hours.

Following my time at the Hall of Fame, I joined the Positively Cleveland CVB Director of Communications for a quick dinner at the Fourth Street Bar and Grill. I say "quick" because the CVB had a ticket for me to attend a Cleveland Indians baseball game at Progressive Field, only a few blocks away, following dinner. The restaurant, located in Cleveland's well-known Corner Alley bowling alley and sports bar on the 4th Street Pedestrian Mall, was rather unique. It was housed in the sixteen-lane, upscale bowling alley which had two sleek bars in addition to the stylish restaurant where we ate. It was definitely unusual, and fun.

After dinner, I walked with thousands of Cleveland baseball fans decked out in their dark blue jerseys trimmed in red and their Chief Wahoo baseball caps to watch the Indians, Bob Hope's favorite baseball team, play the Tampa Bay Rays. Since most of the games I had attended over the years were spent watching the Giants or the Padres in the National League, I looked forward to enjoying another new experience on my trip, an American League game. I thoroughly enjoyed the game as my seat was in a prime location only a few rows from the field, which also was quite different from my usual seats high up in the stands or in the bleachers.

My golf in the Cleveland area, which I was told had over 100 public courses, was at the Sleepy Hollow Golf Course.

Originally built in 1924 as a private course, Sleepy Hollow was one of eight public courses operated by Metroparks, a park district with over 21,000 acres in the Cleveland area dedicated to conservation, education, and recreation. Rated Ohio's #1 municipal course and the #3 public course in the state, Sleepy Hollow had hills to contend with, deep ravines that came into play on thirteen holes, and small, quick-sloping greens. It was a good test of my erratic golf skills.

After Cleveland, I drove to Zanesville, birthplace of noted author Zane Grey. While in Zanesville, I stayed at the Hampton Inn, which was conveniently located just twenty minutes from both Eagle Sticks and Longaberger, the two courses I would play in the area. I had been told about the courses by Bill and Rich Miller (no relation), two brothers who lived in the Zanesville area. I had been paired with them at the Legacy Golf Course when I was in Pinehurst in North Carolina. They told me to call them when I was in Zanesville and said they would join me for a round of golf at Eagle Sticks. I did ... and they did.

Eagle Sticks, built on 150 acres of hilly farmland, was a course where accuracy was more important than power as it had small creeks and/or lakes on seven holes, very few flat lies, nearly 100 sand bunkers, and big, contoured greens. Tees ranging from 4,200 yards from the Reds to 6,500 from the Blues—combined with plush, bentgrass fairways and greens, and mature oak, ash, maple, locust, walnut, and cherry trees—made golfing at Eagle Sticks a memorable experience.

Longaberger Golf Club, which now has a new name, The Virtues Golf club, was a Parkland-style course with rolling fairways, numerous dog legs, panoramic natural beauty, big, fast greens, and a spectacular, 60,000-foot clubhouse. An Arthur Hills design, it had been ranked by *Golfweek* as Ohio's #1 public course every year since 2002. It was built by the Longaberger Basket Company, whose seven-story office building a few miles away was in the shape of a picnic basket, complete with handle. Both the course and Longaberger Basket Company's home office building were spectacular.

Following my fun day of golf at Longaberger, I drove to my next stop, Louisville, Kentucky, home of Churchill Downs and site of world's most famous horse race: the Kentucky Derby.

Kentucky – "Bourbon… and Amazing Quilts"

Although I wasn't scheduled to play golf in Louisville, I was excited to visit the city, thanks to the Louisville Convention and Visitors Bureau. They had arranged for me to stay three nights at the Brown Hotel, a true Louisville landmark that was built in 1923 with lots of marble, high ceilings, and a truly elegant formal dining room, the English Grill.

During my stay, I learned the first person to sign the Brown's guest register, just prior to its formal opening, was former English Prime Minister David Lloyd George, and that actor Victor Mature was once an elevator operator there before earning his fame in Hollywood. I was told other visitors over the years had included the Duke of Windsor, President

Harry Truman, Elizabeth Taylor, Joan Crawford, Gene Autry, jockey Eddie Arcaro, and Louisville native Muhammad Ali. A number of other celebrities, including comedians George Gobel, Dan Rowan and Dick Martin of Laugh-In fame, and musicians Gene Krupa and Clyde McCoy made a name for themselves there before attaining their celebrity status.

While at The Brown, I dined one evening in the English Grill as a guest of the hotel, and what a dinner it was. I chose the hotel's signature item, the Hot Brown, an open-faced turkey and bacon sandwich with Mornay sauce which was created in 1926 as an alternative to the traditional ham and egg enjoyed by guests in the "wee hours" of the morning following a night of dancing. When I had finished my delicious Hot Brown and was about to leave for my room and more computer time, my waitress said I must have a slice of pecan pie and another of the Brown Hotel's signature items, a Bailey's with Kentucky bourbon. She didn't have to spend one moment twisting my arm. I gladly said yes to her suggestion and was very glad I did. What a way to finish off a magnificent evening of dining.

While in Louisville, the Convention and Visitor's Bureau had scheduled a number of tours for me and arranged for me to have breakfast at one of the well-known restaurants in town, the North End Café, where healthy, wholesome food was the order of the day. I was to meet Alex Kruse of Estes Public Relations there for breakfast. When I arrived at the restaurant a bit early, I told the manager I was there to meet Alex Kruse. Much to my surprise, I was told "she is the young lady at the far table."

Alex was not only an excellent PR representative for the Café, but very knowledgeable about Louisville. (Not being a politically correct type, and realizing it is no longer accept-able in some circles to comment about the attractiveness of a member of the opposite sex for fear of being accused of being sexiest, I would like to add this comment) … Alex was a very, very pretty young lady! A nice way to start off a day that would have me touring the Louisville Slugger Museum and Factory, where baseball bats are made for today's big leaguers, and Churchill Downs, "the home of the most famous two minutes in sports."

After my tours, I began my drive to Bowling Green, where I was scheduled to play two courses: Olde Stone, a magnificently groomed private course, and Cross Winds, a Bowling Green municipal course adjacent to the Holiday Inn University Place, where I would be staying. On my drive, I decided to take a detour to visit two of the six bourbon distilleries on the Kentucky Bourbon Trail, Jim Beam in Clermont and Heaven Hill in Bardstown.

At Jim Beam, home of the #1 selling bourbon in the world, I toured the plant including the Rack House, where the clear bourbon ages in new oak barrels to gain its color. I walked through the historic T. Jeremiah Beam home, where three generations of the Beam family lived when they were distilling the family's namesake bourbon; and of course, I visited the sampling room for a few sips of Jim Beam bourbon whiskey. Sipping Jim Beam was like going back in time, as this was my father's favorite bourbon. He had given me a sip one time when I was home from college, when he and my Uncle Tom were making their famous Christmas eggnog.

Wanting to learn more about another Kentucky Bourbon Trail distillery, I next stopped at Heaven Hill, America's largest independent, family owned and operated bourbon producer. There I visited their Bourbon Heritage Center and learned about bourbon pioneers Evan Williams, Kentucky's first distiller, and the Reverend Elijah Craig, the father of bourbon ... and I sampled some of their bourbons in their unique, barrel-shaped testing room.

When I arrived in Bowling Green and asked about the Olde Stone course, I was told PGA pros often practiced there when tuning up for the Masters. After playing it, I understood why. It played to 7,372 yards from the tips, was very hilly, had water and creeks that came into play on several holes, had fairways bordered with three- to four-inch Kentucky Blue Grass rough, and had lightning fast bentgrass greens. I played the Whites at 5,738 yards, which had a slope rating of 128, and found it to be a fun but very difficult course.

I did enjoy hitting a number of the wide, manicured Bermuda grass fairways, but my numerous slices and hooks also had me searching for my golf ball in the treacherous rough on more than one occasion. I settled for four pars en route to my horrendous, near-record-breaking high score of 96, which included two 8's and an 8x. If I hadn't picked up and taken the 8x on the Par 4, 359-yard 12th hole, I might not have broken 100. As it was, my 96 was one shot shy of my highest score on my trip.

The second course I played in Bowling Green was Cross Winds, named the best public course in Bowling Green ten years in a row. Hoping to improve on my previous day's 96 at Olde Stone, I played the 5,300 yard Green Tees, which carried a 114 slope rating. I was able to navigate the totally flat course much better and shot an 83 while avoiding the water that came into play on six holes, as well as most of the largest bunkers in Kentucky, which protected the bentgrass greens.

Following golf, and being quite hungry, I stopped off at the Double Dogs Sports Bar, which was only a block away from my motel. I relaxed there while devouring one of their specialty burgers, a delicious Black Angus Mushroom Swiss Burger, along with one of their local craft beers while watching several baseball games on their multitude of TVs. I liked their variety of burgers, pizza, hot dogs, salads, and beers enough to go off my budget and eat there twice for dinner and once for lunch.

If I had had more time to stay in Bowling Green, I would have loved to have visited the National Corvette Museum, where they had seventy-five classic Corvettes on display. I would have also enjoyed being part of the action at the

National Corvette Museum's Interactive Pit Crew Challenge and Educational Driving Simulators. Other things I would have like to have done would have included treading through an actual Civil War trench on the Civil War Discovery Trail and touring a working dairy farm at Chaney's Dairy Barn, where they make ice cream which had been described by USA Today as the best ice cream in Kentucky. But I had to head for my next Kentucky stop, Paducah, and my lodging at the Fox Briar Inn at RiverPlace, located on Broadway, the most historic block in downtown Paducah.

In Paducah, I played Paxton Park, another excellent, well-maintained municipal course with mature trees, three lakes, and creeks that meandered throughout the course. I was paired with a fellow golfer who had played there for years, including rounds with Champion Tour pros Kenny Perry and Russ Cochran. A par 71 course, Paxton Park had gentle, rolling fairways with lots of mature trees and high-quality greens of Champion Ultra Dwarf Bermuda. I was told this species of Bermuda was replacing bentgrass greens on many courses in the South because it offered bentgrass-quality putting surfaces and yet had Bermuda heat tolerance.

In addition to golf, I drove a freight train on the Railway Museum's simulator, guided a barge down the Ohio River on the River Discovery Center simulator, and visited the 4,000-square-foot Market House Museum with its collection of Paducah artifacts. I also viewed the colorful riverfront panels located next to the river, just a few feet from the

Fox Briar Inn. I had no clue what they were. I only thought they were interesting depictions of Paducah's history until I was told that they were actually floodwalls that protected the city should the river overflow its banks. Not being accustomed to rivers that flood, it was a very intriguing site and concept for me.

I also spent several hours touring the Museum of American Quilters Society, the world's largest and most prestigious museum devoted to quilts and fiber art, which housed more than 150 hand-sewn quilts. If you would have asked me to spend time in a quilt museum prior to actually going there as a guest of the museum, I would've looked at you with a jaundiced eye. The closest I'd ever come to quilts were the ones that Charlene Hauri, an avid quilting neighbor when I lived in El Cajon, California, had made, one for my newborn granddaughter, Ava, and a Christmas quilt for my wife.

I was absolutely blown away by the museum's quilts. They were incredible! There were large ones that must have been ten feet square or more and there were tiny ones. Many were so intricate, they looked more like photographs than my concept of quilts. I was told over 110,000 visitors from all fifty states and from forty or fifty countries around the world come yearly to view the exhibits, which are rotated eight to ten times a year. I definitely recommend a visit to the museum for anyone, not just quilters, as it is an amazing museum.

On my last morning in Paducah, I loaded my car, checked out of my room, and went downstairs to enjoy a hand-dipped ice cream at the Ice Cream Factory. Then I headed to Carbondale in Southern Illinois, my next stop.

Illinois – "Crab Orchard and Kokopelli"

Over the years, I have visited Chicago a number of times for both business and pleasure. I always enjoyed the city's hustle and bustle, its ethnic neighborhoods, and the opportunity to see baseball games at Wrigley Field and Comiskey Park. One time in Chicago, I even had the opportunity to attend an exhibition football game at Soldier Field which pitted the College All-Stars against the reigning champion pro team. (You're right if you think that was a long time ago). While planning my trip, I tried to organize a route that would have me revisiting Chicago. However, it didn't work out that way because a revised driving plan necessitated that I drive to and play golf in Southern Illinois following my stay in Puducah, Kentucky.

After leaving Puducah, I drove to Marion, Illinois, a town of about 17,000 located in Williamson County, an area with a rural presence and a relaxed atmosphere. My inquisitive nature had me asking about the origin of the name of the town. I found out it was named after Revolutionary War hero General Francis "Swamp Fox" Marion who, because of his irregular methods of warfare, is considered to be one of the fathers of modern day guerilla warfare.

Once I arrived in Marion and had my usual fast-food lunch, I checked into the brand new Comfort Inn near the intersection of Interstate 57 and Illinois State 13. When I say brand new, I mean brand new. It had opened only hours before I registered. I was either the second or third person to check in. In spite of the fact that workmen were still completing some finishing touches and I could hear hammers hammering, I enjoyed my stay. I was given an excellent room, had very good complimentary buffet breakfasts each of the four mornings I was there, and was pleased with its location close to both Crab Orchard in Carbondale, and The Links at Kokopelli in Marion, the two courses I was to play.

Crab Orchard, a Par 70 course 6,400 yards from the tips was the home course of the Southern Illinois University golf team. Opened in 1959, it has been noted for its excellent playing conditions throughout its fifty-three-year history. It was a flat course with water that came into play on nine holes and mature oak trees that guarded its Zoysia and Bermuda fairways and its excellent bentgrass greens.

It was obvious that Crab Orchard was a favorite of local golfers, as the course was full when I arrived for my 10:04 tee time and looked to be full for the whole day. With five sets of tees to play from, and the friendliness of the staff, it appeared to me that Crab Orchard offered a great opportunity for a fun round of golf for beginners as well as low handicappers.

Following golf, I grabbed a quick hot dog and Diet Coke and headed off to a three o'clock appointment at the Nissan dealership to find out why I was hearing a banging noise coming from the back of my trustee 2004 Nissan Maxima. I wasn't sure what was wrong when I went to the dealership, but they found the problem, explained what it was, and in less than an hour, they had it fixed. Evidently, somewhere along the way—or possibly from ten years of use—my back left fender guard had come loose and, while driving at speeds of forty-five to fifty-five miles per hour, would vibrate and bang against my back left tire. After paying my bill of $162.84, I was on my way with a new left fender guard, no more highway noise, and a relived feeling. I had been worried that I had a major problem that would drain my budget. As it turned out, the $162.84 bill, except for one oil change and lube job, was the only car maintenance charge I had during my 21,503 miles on the road.

The second course I played, The Links at Kokopelli, a Par 72 course which stretched out to over 7,000 yards from its back tees, was practically out the back door from the

Comfort Inn. I got to sleep in until my noisy alarm woke me from a sound sleep at eight in the morning. Since I normally was up by seven every day, and my tee time wasn't until 9:40, setting the alarm to give me an extra hour sleep was something I did happily.

Listed as #3 in Illinois by *Golf Magazine* in its 2006 publication "America's Best Places You Can Play," Kokopelli had plenty of character. Accurate tee shots to sloping fairways were a necessity in order to avoid the course's abundance of deep bunkers. A good putting stroke on Kokopelli's smooth, fast, and undulating greens was also an absolute must. I finished my round with only two three putts and felt some degree of satisfaction.

I had the good fortune to play my round with a young girl who was interning at the club. She had played the course quite often as a member of her school's golf team and was able to give me hints as to how to play the holes. She beat me handily. Oh, to be young again!

In addition to golf, we talked about the 100-degree days the area was having and the drought conditions in Southern Illinois and other parts of the Midwest. I learned a lot about the perils of farming as well as golf during our round. As the daughter of a farmer in the area, she was familiar with several families who were near bankruptcy because of the drought and the fact that they didn't have crop insurance. Evidently, the farmers she referred to hadn't renewed their insurance because they had never experienced a drought of this magnitude and felt comfortable without insurance. Without even knowing the farmers I was told about, I felt for them.

Both Crab Orchard and Kokopelli were in good shape, considering the lack of rain and the high temperatures. I enjoyed them both and was glad that I had the opportunity to not only play the courses but to get a feel for areas of Southern Illinois I had previously never visited.

Missouri – "Golf and Great Shows"

For years, I had heard and read about Branson, Missouri, known as the "Live Music Show Capital of the World." I knew that millions of people, both young and old, had been entertained at shows in its more than fifty live-performance theaters. I wanted to experience Branson in person. But shows weren't the only thing that had me thinking about Branson. When I heard Branson also had excellent golf courses, I worked hard to arrange my golf odyssey to include a visit there.

I made arrangements to play two of the well-known courses, Thousand Hills at the Thousand Hills Golf Resort and Murder Rock Golf and Country Club. I chose both courses after reviewing their various awards. Thousand Hills had been listed in *Golf Digest's* 2008/2009 "Best Places to Play" edition, and was named the Best Branson Golf Course in 2009 and 2010. Murder Rock was also an award-winner, having been selected as one of the top five courses in Missouri and being awarded "Best Courses You Can Play" status by *Golfweek Magazine*.

The Thousand Hills course, which featured zoysia fairways and Crenshaw bentgrass greens, was a Par 64 course at only a little over 5,100 yards from the back tees. I thought it might be an easy course because of its length and the fact it had nine Par 3s. I would have known better if I had seen the slope rating of 126. It was a challenging course with creeks to avoid, small lakes to hit over, very few flat lies, sloping fairways, sizeable greenside bunkers protecting elevated undulating greens, and two Par 3s that were more than 200 yards.

The course had only one Par 5, the 18th hole, and it was a doozy … 533 yards with a creek running the entire length of the hole, first on the left side of the fairway, and then, after crossing the fairway, all the way to and back of the green. The 18th hole was a true test—and I flunked! I sliced two balls into the creek and had to sink a fifteen-foot putt to avoid a quadruple bogey.

Murder Rock, designed by John Daly, was founded in 2007 on one of the highest points in the county. It is now known as Buffalo Ridge Valley Golf Course and is part of a two-course complex, along with the Buffalo Ridge Springs Golf Course, formerly called Branson Creek Golf Course. Both courses were purchased in 2013 by Johnny Morris, founder of Bass Pro Shops.

In addition to being a good test of golf with an abundance of uphill, blind tee shots to wide fairways, Murder Rock—as it was then known—had lovely, scenic views of the rolling hills and valleys in the Branson area. It was noted for its smooth and quick bentgrass greens that had breaks that ranged from subtle to dramatic. In 2009 and 2010, *Golfweek* listed the course in the "Top Fifty Courses Women Can Play" and in the top five "Courses You Can Play in the State of Missouri."

Other notable championship-length courses in Branson included the Payne Stewart Golf Club, which was relatively new at the time I was there, and the Ledgestone Golf Course. Although not a championship-length course, I was told one other "don't miss" course was the nine-hole Par 3 course, The Top of the Rock. Also owned by Bass Pro Shop founder Johnny Morris, in 2014 it was the site of the Champion Tour's Bass Pro Shop Legends of Golf tournament, the first-ever Par 3 course to be included in a PGA Tour event. Morris spent eight years designing his world-class golfing facility with the assistance of golf legends Jack Nicklaus, Tom Watson, and Arnold Palmer. The Nicklaus Design Group designed the course. Tom Watson was instrumental in the design and development of the 70,000-square-foot putting complex known as "Himalayas" and Arnold Palmer designed the practice facility, which included a 150-year-old barn. "Arnie's Barn" was disassembled and brought from Palmer's backyard in Latrobe, Pennsylvania and rebuilt, plank by plank, at Top of the Rock. Although I didn't have a chance to see it, the barn evidently contains not only historic photos and memorabilia from Palmer's career but also a world-class pro shop.

While in Branson, I had a complimentary, three-night stay in a very tastefully decorated, privately owned condominium at the Thousand Hills Golf Resort, a large complex with over 300 units including premium golf-front condominiums, patio homes, and opulent, romantic log cabins.

My short, three-day stay was busy, so I didn't have time to check out the other amenities at the resort, which included seven indoor/outdoor pools, tennis, shuffleboard and basketball courts, a children's play area, hot tubs, an exercise facility, a meeting facility for groups up to 200, and lake condos at nearby Table Rock Lake. (I enjoyed Thousand Hills so much, we chose it as the location for a 2015 Thanksgiving family reunion).

For shoppers, Branson had everything from soup to nuts … from souvenir and t-shirt shops to outlet stores. The largest outlet, Tanger Outlets, had over sixty-five brands and designers. Its slogan was "Seriously Chic Always in Style … up to 70 Percent Off." I didn't care about being "Seriously Chic" but I did enjoy the hefty discounts on the few items I bought there. Another favorite place for shoppers that I visited was Branson Landing, the downtown, outdoor, pedestrian mall which was anchored by Bass Pro Shop and the Belk department store.

Live entertainment shows originally brought Branson fame and fortune, with entertainers from all genres performing there. I only had time for one show, so I chose to see The Haygoods, a highly entertaining show performed by five brothers and a sister who had been recognized four times as Branson Entertainers of the Year. They were performing in their twentieth year in Branson when I was there. They played more than twenty instruments and sang and danced with skills that everyone in the audience, no matter what age, thoroughly enjoyed.

Branson was a fun city with wonderful shows, excellent golf courses, dining to fit any taste, and terrific resorts like Thousand Hill Golf Resort, Big Cedar Lodge, and the Keeter Center at College of the Ozarks. For the budget-minded, hundreds of motels offered discounted rates.

A word of advice: When you visit Branson, make sure your GPS is working, as it is a hilly city with lots of intersections that make it is easy to get lost. Try to avoid State Highway 76, the very busy main artery that runs from downtown through the heart of the entertainment area. I found it beneficial to use one of Branson's three major bypasses—the Red, the Blue, or the Yellow—all of which connect at various points with Highway 76.

Now that my wife and I live only four hours south of Branson in Hot Springs Village, Arkansas. —see Week 31 and Week 51—we have returned twice to Branson to enjoy the winning combination of great golf and great shows.

Arkansas – "HSV... A Golfer's Paradise"

My original plan was to visit and play golf in Hot Springs, Arkansas, located about an hour and a half west of Little Rock, Arkansas' capital. I wanted to go there in early February after my stay in Baton Rouge, Louisiana and then swing down to Mississippi. However, my plan didn't work as I had hoped. I was thwarted by the hundreds of thoroughbred horses racing at the Oaklawn Racetrack in Hot Springs.

In January, I contacted the Convention and Visitors Bureau in Hot Springs while in Texas and explained my interest in coming to Hot Springs. When I asked about the availability of complimentary accommodations, I was told none were available as it was the middle of the thoroughbred racing season at Oaklawn and the hotels and motels were booked solid. It was suggested I call Hot Springs Village, about thirty minutes north of Hot Springs and an hour and a half west of Little Rock.

Chances are, unless you have lived in Arkansas or a nearby state, you've probably never heard of Hot Springs Village, even though it is the largest gated community in the U.S. I certainly didn't have a clue about it. When I called and spoke with Dannet Botkin, the Village's marketing director at the time, I learned the Village was located in a 26,000-acre pine and hardwood forest and that it had eleven lakes, and nine golf courses. She also explained that, although it wasn't a fifty-five-and-over retirement community, retirees made up about 80 percent of its resident population.

Dannet told me that, unfortunately, the Village—like Hot Springs—couldn't provide complimentary accommodations because of the busy racing season. Following my theory that "It's a Mark of Leadership to Adjust," I revised my February schedule and planned my Arkansas visit for late July, when I was going to be on my western swing.

On July 25, after a four-hour drive from Branson—partially on well-groomed freeways and partially on curvy roads through the spectacularly scenic Ozark National Forest—I checked into The Village Inn, which is located just outside the west gate of Hot Springs Village. I had contacted Dannet in June, and although no complimentary accommodations were available, she was able to secure a room for me at The Village Inn at a discounted rate. The Inn was conveniently located near the Sonic Drive-In, where I was able to enjoy quick and inexpensive fast-food lunches, and The Italian House & Grill, where I splurged a bit one night and savored an excellent Fettuccine Bolognese dinner with a glass of Chianti.

In June, I had also contacted John Paul, the Hot Springs Village Director of Golf, and he arranged for me to play four of the nine courses in the village. Two of the courses, Granada and Isabella, were rated in the top ten in the state. A third top-ten course within the village, which I didn't have time to play, was Diamante Country Club, a ClubCorp private club.

In addition to Granada and Isabella, I also played the Balboa and Cortez courses and viewed two others. Each one was a scenic beauty with ponds, lake and mountain views, beautiful, wide manicured fairways, dog legs to maneuver, and numerous large, elevated, bentgrass greens. I was very surprised and very pleased with the condition of the courses. All the courses, which had been designed and built by the same golf course architectural firm during the period from 1972 to 2004, were in excellent shape, considering the summer's unusually high temperatures and drought conditions. And, amazingly, there didn't seem to be any duplication of holes on any of the courses I played or viewed.

When I arrived in the village, a suggestion was made that I call Jeff Hollansworth of RE/MAX Real Estate and ask him about the village. When I called him, Jeff offered to take me on a tour of the village. During our two-hour tour, he explained that, besides the beautiful lakes and golf courses, village residents and vacationers enjoyed tennis, pickleball, basketball, swimming, kayaking, fishing, bicycling, working out at the Fitness Center, hiking on the more than twenty-four miles of trails, taking in plays and concerts at the village's 654 seat state-of-the-art auditorium, dancing with live bands and DJs, and participating in the Village's more than 150 clubs, churches, and organizations.

If I sound like a sales agent for Hot Springs Village, I assure you, I'm not. I just loved my visit there. In fact, I loved it so much, I moved to Hot Springs Village on December 11, 2012 following my trip to Hawaii to visit and play golf in the last state on my golf odyssey.

If you are curious about Hot Springs Village, let me make two suggestions: Google youtube.com/hotspringsvillage and/or go to the Village's website www.hsvpoa.org. You will see why Hot Springs Village is thought of as "A Golfer's Paradise."

Oklahoma – "Drillers and Brother Harry"

As a Southern Californian, I wasn't used to the unusually hot 100 to 105-degree weather I was experiencing as I headed to my next stop, Tulsa, Oklahoma, following six days in Hot Springs Village, Arkansas. I was weathering the heat fine because I was quite comfortable driving my trusty 2004 Nissan Maxima with the air conditioning on full blast. However, I was a bit concerned about what effect the heat would have on my car, which had been so dependable thus far on my trip. Would the air conditioning go out from overuse? Would the engine overheat and leave me stranded along the road, hoping AAA would respond quickly to my emergency call? Fortunately, my fears were baseless. My drive to Tulsa was uneventful, although I have to say I was relieved when I pulled into the driveway of the downtown

DoubleTree Hotel, where complimentary accommodations had been arranged for me.

I checked in and schlepped my suitcase, computer bag, and briefcase to my room using the handy bellman's cart. I seldom used a bellman, even if one was available, in order not to deplete my meager budget with a tip. I actually explained this to the DoubleTree bellman and he said he totally understood, since he, too, was a golfer.

I enjoyed my lunch while sitting at the desk in my room. I was famished, as I hadn't had much breakfast, so half of the twelve-inch turkey sandwich and half of the Diet Coke I had purchased at a Subway along the way were welcome treats. I wanted to eat the other half of the sandwich, but I had to save it for dinner that night. At this point, I was wishing my food budget could have been double my self-imposed eight to ten dollars a day.

While in Tulsa, I played two courses: Forest Ridge, a public course in a master-planned community in nearby Broken Arrow, and the Tulsa Country Club, a private course designed by A.W. Tillinghast. At both courses, because of the extreme heat during my rounds, it was hit the ball, drink water, hit the ball, drink water. It seemed to work fine. I shot 82 at Forest Ridge with four birdies and an 83 at the Tulsa Country Club. These scores pleased me to no end, since both were on Par 70, championship-length courses.

Forest Ridge had a four-and-a-half-star designation from *Golf Digest*, had been rated in the Best Courses You Can Play category by *Golfweek Magazine*, and was one of the top daily-fee courses in Oklahoma. It was a flat course. However, the tree-lined fairways, strategically placed bunkers, water which came into play on four holes, and swirling breezes made it anything but easy.

I was paired with a very pleasant golfer who introduced himself as Brother Harry. Questioning him about his name, I learned he and his wife had a counseling ministry specializing in marriage and family counseling. I teased him that some of his counseling must've been on the golf course, as he was a very good golfer.

When we finished a most enjoyable round that had us laughing and talking, he handed me a fifty-dollar Outback Steakhouse gift card. He said that often couples he counseled gave him presents of this nature, and he wanted me to have it as his way of thanking me for my support of the Wounded Warrior Project. Although his gift was totally appreciated, I tried turning it down. Brother Harry wouldn't have any part of it. He insisted that I take it and enjoy a nice lunch or dinner at Outback. I used it that night and had one of the few steak dinners I had enjoyed in nearly seven months. I devoured one of Outback's famous Blooming Onions along with a divine, eight-ounce filet mignon and a baked potato, salad, and dessert. Brother Harry's example of generosity and kindness brought home to me why the "Pay It Forward" concept is such an admirable thing to do.

The second course I played, the Tulsa Country Club, was the oldest course in Tulsa, having been founded in 1908. For one of the few times on my tour, I didn't play a complete round with another golfer. I played the front nine with a member and alone on the back nine. I was told it was just too hot for most members. In spite of the heat and the summer-long drought, the course was in excellent shape following a restoration completed the previous year by acclaimed golf course architect Rees Jones. It had new greens, fairways, and tee boxes, as well as revised bunkers and a new irrigation system. I never did find out how much the renovation cost, but it must have been in the millions.

On the way back to the DoubleTree after playing the Tulsa Country Club, I decided to drive through downtown Tulsa to view the art deco buildings from the 1920s and '30s I had heard about. I also wanted to check out the seventy-six-foot-high Golden Driller, one of the tallest free-standing statues in the world. It had been made as a salute to the oil industry drillers that helped make Oklahoma the "oil capital of the world" in the early 1900s.

Once back at the hotel, I showered, changed clothes, and was off to ONEOK Field, the baseball home of the Tulsa Drillers, the AA affiliate of the Colorado Rockies. I had been invited to join a group from the Tulsa Metro Chamber of Commerce and the Visit Tulsa Convention and Visitors Bureau who were going to the ballpark to enjoy a Texas League game. Loving baseball, and thoroughly enjoying minor-league baseball parks because of their proximity to the field and the players, I was delighted to be invited. When I got to the ballpark and found out that I would be watching the game from a VIP box, which had both indoor and outdoor seating, I was thrilled.

Although it was 103 degrees, I spent about half my time in the comfortable outdoor seats. I wanted to get a feel for what the local fans went through to see a ballgame in such heat. The other half of my time was spent indoors enjoying the wide array of food and beverages. Since most of the ballgames I had been to in California were either at the major league stadiums of the San Diego Padres or the San Francisco Giants, where on a hot day the temperature might get into the 80s, this was a new experience for me. It showed me that Tulsa baseball fans, despite the heat, were really good baseball fans. It was a fun evening.

My last day in Tulsa, I wrapped up my visit with a private tour of the Gilcrease Museum. Although no one has ever considered me a museum devotee, my visit to the Gilcrease was one I thoroughly enjoyed. It featured one of the nation's largest and most comprehensive collections of fine arts and artifacts of the American West, as well as an unparalleled collection of Native American art, historical manuscripts, maps, and documents of the Americas. I was particularly intrigued with one of the most significant documents in the Gilcrease collection, a letter written in 1512 describing life on Hispaniola (now Haiti and the

Dominican Republic). The letter was the oldest existing letter written in the Western Hemisphere.

Following my tour of the Gilcrease, I grabbed a fast-food lunch and was off to Topeka, Kansas.

WEEK 33 – AUGUST 4

Kansas – "Around the Lake and on the Prairie"

When I arrived in Topeka, late in the afternoon after a four-hour drive from Tulsa, I checked into my comfortable and well-appointed room at the Ramada Topeka Downtown Hotel and Convention Center just off Interstate 70. I quickly realized my complimentary stay, which had been arranged for me by Visit Topeka Inc., was going to be very relaxing.

Prior to visiting Topeka, I didn't know much about the city other than that it was the capital of Kansas. I had the feeling that I would learn a great deal on my second day in Topeka as I was scheduled to have a meeting and lunch with Shalyn Murphy, Communications and Marketing Director for Visit Topeka Inc.

Realizing I didn't want to feel like a total dunce with little or no knowledge about Topeka when I lunched with Shalyn, I grabbed a quick dinner at the nearby McDonalds, hightailed it back to my room, and did a little homework via the Internet to find out more about the city. I learned that Topeka was the site of the Brown vs. Board of Education National Historic Site and museum, honoring the 1954 Supreme Court decision which mandated desegregation in schools. I read that Topeka had a 160-acre park which was home to the zoo and a rose garden with more than 400 varieties of roses. I learned that Heartland Park Topeka, one of the premier racing facilities in the US, hosted close to 275 events each year including the NHRA (National Hot Rod Association) Summer Nationals. I also read with great interest about the Lake Shawnee Golf Course, where I was scheduled to play the next day. I hit the sack early because getting up at five a.m. for my 6:30 tee time wasn't going to allow me much time to sleep.

Lake Shawnee Golf Course was a county-owned course built around a man-made recreational lake. Although only 6,300-yards from the tips, it was challenging because of its many trees, up and down sloping fairways, and water that came into play on eight holes. I particularly liked the Par 5 515-yard fifteenth hole because it required three types of shots to reach the green: an accurate uphill tee shot, a blind second shot over a hill, and a delicate downhill third shot to a small green bordering the lake. The course, which had zoysia fairways and bentgrass greens, was in good shape considering the sweltering heat and drought that was sweeping the area. Playing alongside the lake on holes that had breathtaking views of Lake Shawnee made for a fun day of golf.

Firekeeper, the second course I played, was located in Mayetta, thirty miles north of Topeka. Owned by the Prairie Band of the Potowatomi Nation, it was designed by four-time PGA winner Notah Begay III in partnership with ASGCA architect Jeffrey D. Bauer. At the time it was built, it was the only course in the nation designed by a full-blooded Native American on Native American soil. It opened in 2011 to great reviews. It was named the #1 Public Access Course in Kansas, the #9 New Best Course in the US, and the #18 Best Casino Course. Shortly before I played it, it was also named in the Top 100 Resort Courses in the US.

The Par 72 beauty, which had five sets of tees, opened with seven holes on the open prairie and finished up with eleven holes that played in more wooded areas. Besides bunkers that seem to attract my shots, it had fescue rough, native prairie grass, and a few creeks that wound through the back nine. Accurate shots to the good-size and fast bentgrass greens were important, particularly the one shared by the Par 4 first hole and the Par 5 sixth hole. I wish I could say that I hit them all of the time. I wish I could say most of the time. Actually, as I remember, besides the Par 3s, I hit only three greens in regulation.

When I played Firekeeper, I was given accommodations at the Prairie Band's Resort and Casino, just one half mile away. It had beautiful rooms, three restaurants, a small pool under a waterfall, a casino with 1,100 slot machines and numerous table games ... and I was able to drive a mile or so down the road to observe a herd of 200 head of buffalo grazing on 420 acres of tribal land.

Because of my tight schedule, I didn't have a chance to see all of things I would've liked to have seen in Topeka and the surrounding area. I would've enjoyed visiting the former home and museum of Charles Curtis, the only US Vice President of Native American descent. Also, I would have loved seeing the thirty military aircraft from World War I to the present day at the Combat Air Museum. I wish I'd been able to visit Gage Park's 160 acres which contains the Topeka Zoo and the aforementioned rose garden. I would have enjoyed taking the mile-long scenic train ride through the heart of the park, and I could have revived the kid in me by riding on the historic carousel, built in 1908.

Although I'm not a coffee drinker, I would also have liked visiting PT's Coffee Roasting Company, which first opened in 1933 as a single coffee shop in Topeka. Since I love the smell of coffee beans and ground coffee, but do not drink coffee, I would have liked to have seen, heard, and asked about coffee roasting. Considering PT's Coffee Roasting Company had been recognized as Roaster of the Year by *Roast Magazine*, I figured I could have learned a lot about coffee, maybe even including why I didn't like the taste of brewed coffee, even though practically every adult I have ever known loved coffee

A side note about Topeka: I now may have a chance to do all the things mentioned above that I didn't have a chance to do. Myrna, my bride of two years, and I are beginning to visit Topeka periodically as her daughter, Cheryl, son-in-law Joe, and grandsons James, Jack, and Nathan live there. Myrna's son-in-law, Joe Hishmeh, is the Senior Pastor of Topeka's Fellowship Bible Church.

Iowa – "Withered Corn and Sand in the City"

D riving from Topeka to Iowa City—on my way to play golf at Amana Colonies in Amana and Brown Deer in Coralville, two communities in the Iowa City metropolitan area—I saw miles and miles of corn fields. As a California non-farm boy, my dealings with corn were pretty much limited to picking up an ear or two at a local supermarket. Seeing this much corn was a new experience for me. Unfortunately, due to the drought the nation was going through at the time, particularly in the Midwest farm belt, most of the fields looked dry, the corn stocks short, and the ears decimated.

I decided to get a closer look at the withering corn when I stopped for an inexpensive, fast-food lunch at a Dairy Queen located next to a cornfield. I walked over to the cornfield, pulled back the silk on an ear of corn, and saw that the kernels were dried and shriveled up. After seeing this type of devastation, which undoubtedly was similar through the cornfield, my hope was that the farmers had crop insurance, as their crop damage was going to be significant.

While in the Iowa City area, I stayed at the Suburban Extended Stay hotel in Coralville, a great place for me as it had a complete kitchen, which I used to prepare my soup and salad dinners. It also had an excellent fitness facility, which I looked at but didn't use, because rigorous exercise and Chuck Miller have never been synonymous terms. It did have complimentary, high speed internet access which allowed me to spend needed and quality time on my trusty laptop, connecting with my family.

I also stayed at the Brown Street Inn, a delightful B&B in downtown Iowa City. It was a cottage-style mansion with six wonderfully decorated bedrooms including a large third floor suite, which surprisingly, I was given. (Love those CVB people and their connections). I enjoyed the Inn's full continental breakfast; the opportunity to visit with Mark Ruggeberg, one of the very knowledgeable and helpful innkeepers; and the Inn's convenient walking distance to both downtown Iowa City and the University of Iowa.

Both the Suburban Extended Stay Hotel and the Brown Street Inn were conveniently located near The Amana Colonies Golf Club in Amana, and Brown Deer Golf Club in

Coralville, which saved me extra driving time and allowed me to put fewer gas-eating miles on my speedometer.

The Amana Colonies Golf Club, which opened in 1989, was masterfully carved through a hilly forest of stately white oaks. I enjoyed the layout, which was described to me as "a course designed to preserve the natural features of the land." Even with the challenge of an abundance of trees, which lined almost every fairway from tee to green, water on seven holes, left and right doglegs, and numerous blind shots, I had an enjoyable day playing my round with Assistant Pro Clayton Farnsworth, who guided me shot by shot, hole by hole.

With five sets of tees, the Amana Colonies course could be played from 5,200 yards to 6,800 yards. I played it from 5,800 yards, and except for my errant slices, which found the trees or water, I did okay ... meaning I broke 90. After playing the course, I understood why it had received national awards, including being voted in 1990 as one of *Golf Magazine's* "Top Ten Best New Public Courses in the Country."

The second course I played was Brown Deer Golf Club in Coralville. It had two totally different nines. The front nine was open, with wide fairways, while the back nine was narrower and considerably more wooded. It had four sets of tees ranging from 4,600 to 6,300 yards, bentgrass fairways and greens, and water which came into play on six holes. My favorite hole at Brown Deer was 393-yard par 4 eighteenth hole, a dog leg right with a lake running on the right from tee to green. I liked it because it was a true risk-reward hole. I risked ... but wasn't rewarded.

The course record 63 was held by Head Professional Sean McCarty who had recently won the Iowa Section PGA Professional Championship. I had the opportunity to play my round at Brown Deer with him. After watching Sean hit super long drives, move the ball left to right or right to left as needed, hit crisp iron shots that went higher than mine went long, and sink curling putts, I understood why he had been a Big Ten All American, had qualified for the U.S. Open in 2003, and had been the Iowa State Player of the Year 2007 through 2009. In addition to his golf skills, which I watched enviously, he was a friendly and helpful host. I felt very fortunate that he took time out from his Head Professional duties to play Brown Deer with me.

One evening while in Iowa City, I walked the short six blocks from the Brown Street Inn to downtown, where I ate an inexpensive spaghetti dinner at one of the many downtown restaurants and got a feel for the city whose slogan was "Small Town Atmosphere, Big City Choices." During dinner, I read various brochures touting the city and was intrigued by all the listed activities available throughout the city. I surmised that the city's slogan was "right on."

The next day, before leaving for Wisconsin, I drove back to town and enjoyed walking around the "Sand in the City" festival, which featured live entertainment, artist booths, a giant sand box for kids to play in, and teams from local organizations building sand sculptures representing well-known, recognizable structures like the Great Wall of China and the Taj Mahal. I felt as if I was back in Coronado, California watching the sand sculpture contests that take place annually on the white, sandy ocean beaches near the famous Del Coronado Hotel.

Being the baseball fan that I am, I was disappointed I didn't have time during my visit to the Hawkeye State for a quick drive to Cedar Rapids to see the Cedar Rapids Kernels play a minor league baseball game. But I had to drive to Wisconsin, my next state. Maybe next time.

Wisconsin – "Golf, Bowling and Go Carts"

Busy! That one word accurately describes my stay in the Eau Claire/Chippewa Falls area of Wisconsin, the thirty-fifth state on my tour. Three hotels, golf on three different length courses, plus go-cart racing, mini bowling, and riding in bumper cars kept me on the go the four days I was there.

The three courses I played were the nine-hole Ojibwa Golf Course and the eighteen-hole Lake Hallie Golf Club in Chippewa Falls, both only minutes from downtown Eau Claire, and the Hickory Hills executive course in Eau Claire. All three were relaxed country courses and, although they were not what the pros would call tour-level courses, all three were in good condition and fun to play. Locals and visitors alike were playing the courses because they offered sufficient challenges yet could be played by golfers of all ages and skill levels.

The nine-hole par 35 Ojibwa Golf Course, built in 1929, had tree-lined fairways and very small greens, the norm for courses of that time. It had two Par 3s, a short 112-yarder that required a shot through a narrow opening and a tough uphill 182-yarder which called for a near blind shot to the green. It also had six Par 4s, the longest being 404 yards, and one 450-yard Par 5. It wasn't an easy course by any means. However, with tees ranging from 2,400 to just under 2,900 yards, it was definitely a course that both beginners and low handicappers could enjoy.

After I enjoyed my two hours on the course, I followed my round by walking less than a chip shot away from the ninth green to check out Jim Bob's Pizza, located inside the on-site, eight-lane bowling alley that was part of the Ojibwa Golf and Bowl complex. Experiencing this low-key combination golf and bowling facility reminded me I was in a small town. I loved it!

After Ojibwa, I drove a few miles to play the eighteen hole Par 70 Lake Hallie Golf Course, a rather short course with three sets of tees ranging from a little over 4,700 yards to just under 5,900 yards. Because of its many trees, water on eleven holes, and tough, well-placed fairway and greenside bunkers, like Ojibwa, it played more difficult than its yardage suggested. I played from the Whites at

5,354 yards with local golfers who had course knowledge. This was helpful, as learning where and how to avoid water hazards—plus being told how to approach and putt on the small, sloping greens—definitely helped my game. I shot 41 on both nines for a reasonable round of 82, considering I managed to dump tee shots into water hazards on both the first and eighth holes.

While playing the eighth hole, in addition to dumping my last TaylorMade ball into the lake, which ran along the length of the hole, I was able to watch fishermen gliding smoothly by while casting their lines in the lake. As I enjoyed my golf game and the relaxed and fun golfers I was playing with, I thought it would be a great outing if I could treat my golfing buddies back home to a trip to Chippewa Falls, where we could go fishing on Lake Hallie in the morning and play golf on the Lake Hallie course in the afternoon. We could even take time out for lunch and a few of the local Leinenkugel beers in between. Short of winning the lottery, I can only dream of such an event.

My third course was Hickory Hills, a Par 63, very walkable executive course four miles south of Eau Claire, which was geared toward the recreational golfer. Voted "The Best Golf Course in the Chippewa Valley" every year since 2003, just like both Ojibwa and Lake Hallie, it had a very friendly and relaxed atmosphere. With a 98 slope rating from the 4,168 yard back tees, it was definitely a family-oriented course.

After playing the three courses, I reflected that often golfers, including myself, get pretty jaded about courses we play or want to play. These three courses brought me back to reality. They made me realize once again that golf is a game that can be played and enjoyed at pretty much any age and by golfers of all skill levels. The golfers we watch on TV are so intense that I'm not sure they have as much fun, because of their aggressive and competitive nature, as do beginners or high handicappers who play courses for sheer enjoyment and the opportunity to enjoy the outdoors.

This realization was definitely brought home to me at Lake Hallie and Hickory Hills, where I watched golfers of all ages and skill levels play, and at Ojbiwa, where I saw families with little tykes as young as maybe six or seven years old enjoying the day playing (and attempting to play) the great game of golf. The children's awkward swings, their putts that were off line, and the smiles in the parents' eyes when a good shot was made, all reminded me of my early days playing golf with my dad.

While in the Eau Claire area, I stayed at three different properties: the Metropolis Resort and the Grandstay Residential Suites Hotel in Eau Claire, and the Holiday Inn Express in Chippewa Falls. All three were excellent with large bedrooms and/or suites, continental or full breakfasts, and convenient locations only minutes from downtown Eau Claire and the Ojibwa, Lake Hallie, and Hickory Hills golf courses. And, all three had free, high-speed Wi-Fi, which saved me money while giving me quick access to the Internet. I was very pleased with the accommodations and golf the Visit Eau Claire CVB had arranged for me.

The Metropolis Resort was definitely designed with families and business travelers in mind. It had excellent amenities in the rooms and suites. With few exceptions, my room at the resort had to be the biggest room I stayed in on my entire trip. A large family could have stayed in it very comfortably.

My granddaughters, Shanna, Ava, and Mia—who were sixteen, seven, and six at the time I was in Wisconsin—would have loved the Action City Fun Center and Indoor Chaos Waterpark at the resort. It had 55,000 square feet of games, indoor go-carts rides, outdoor sprint cars, a climbing wall, laser tag, batting cages, mini bowling, bumper cars, mini-golf, an indoor water slide, a lazy river to float on, multiple activity pools, a hot tub, and food at the Splash Bar and Grill.

The Action City Fun Center was definitely oriented to family entertainment. But I have to tell you that its games and rides were also fun for me. I had a ball riding the go carts, swinging at pitches in the batting cages, playing laser tag, mini bowling, riding in bumper cars, and pretending I was competing in a NASCAR race while speeding around the outdoor sprint car track.

I also enjoyed the Chaos Waterpark, the world's only comic book-themed park, where I slid down slides at what seemed to me like lightning speeds, floated around the lazy river, and walked the line on the ropes course. The Metropolis brochure that I picked up said, "With so much to do there is no chance of getting bored." That was definitely the case. I was quite pleased that both the resort manager and the sales manager took kindly to me and gave me passes to enjoy both the Action City Fun Center and the Chaos Waterpark as a guest of the resort.

The Eau Claire/Chippewa Falls area had fun, relaxed golf and fun places to stay. It was a busy time for me, full of diverse activities that added to some of the most unusual and memorable experiences I had during my year on the road.

Minnesota – "Cargill and Alex"

My visit to Minnesota, officially named "L'Etoile du Nord"—which is French for "Star of the North"—and known to Minnesotans as "The North Star State" or "The Land of Ten Thousand Lakes," had me playing two distinctly different golf courses. My first course was Rush Creek in Maple Grove, just minutes from downtown Minneapolis. My second course was Geneva Golf Club in the Alexandria Lakes area, about two hours northwest of Minneapolis. Rush Creek was built on 260 acres of lush, rolling terrain, whereas the Geneva Golf Club's twenty-seven holes were built on an open prairie with few trees but plenty of natural grass and ponds. They did have one thing in common: both were built by families.

Rush Creek was built by members of the Cargill Company family in 1996 to give local and visiting players the opportunity to play a private-style course at public course prices. It definitely looked, felt, and played like a private course. In addition to its marvelous design—which included natural grasses, lakes, ponds, and marshes in what was described to me as "a scenic natural habitat"—it had a large, highly attractive and well-appointed clubhouse, which housed a pro shop, restaurant, and meeting rooms.

I played the course's 137 slope rated 6,100-yard Silver Tees in steady winds with twenty- to thirty-mile-an-hour gusts. Playing in these windy conditions, which I was told were quite unusual, gave me an inkling as to what tour players periodically are confronted with during their quest for fame and fortune. As to my score, let's just say if there had been a booby prize in my foursome, I would have won, hands down. I had to play hard to shoot 94.

After playing Rush Creek, I drove Highway 94 to Alexandria, known to local Minnesotans by its nickname, "Alex," to play the 27-hole Geneva Golf Club. The course was owned and operated by Gary and Barb Thompson, who built and opened it in the spring of 2000. Its three nines—the Ponds, the Island, and the Marsh—were built on open prairie with few trees but plenty of natural grass and ponds … lots of ponds. I was fortunate to have the opportunity to play eighteen of the twenty-seven holes with two local golfers: Dennis Anhalt, the News Director at KXRA Radio in Alexandria, and Joe Korkowski, Marketing Strategist for KXRA's parent company, Paradis Broadcasting.

With Dennis and Joe's guidance as to where to aim to avoid the omnipresent water, and a somewhat easier course to contend with, I shot an 84 with eight pars and two birdies on the Marsh/Island eighteen. "Coulda, woulda, shoulda" been better, but two double bogeys and a triple bogey snowman had me reeling. After the eighteenth hole, I grabbed my usual quick and inexpensive golf course lunch of a hot dog and Diet Coke and then went out and played the Ponds nine. It was well-named, as it had a lot of ponds.

The highlight of my round on the Ponds nine came on the final hole. I noticed a group of twelve attractive women standing near the Geneva Lodge, adjacent to the green. They noticed me and began to point. I realized quickly that they weren't beckoning to me but, in fact, were pointing at my highly colorful, Loudmouth golf pants. Being the shy type of person I am, I quickly finished putting, hopped into my golf cart, and drove over to them to say hello.

I explained that I was a golf and travel writer on a 50-week, 50-state golf tour. I told how Loudmouth had given me several pair of wild-but-fun pants and golf shorts to wear. Then, when asked, I posed for a photo with them. They wanted to show their husbands, who were on their way up from the Minneapolis area for a weekend of couples golf, a photo of them with "their new California friend." Since all of us were staying in the lodge's spacious two-bedroom suites, which had full kitchens and patios overlooking the golf course, and having dinner later at the course's Geneva Bar and Grill, I had the opportunity to meet the husbands. Unlike their wives, they didn't point or ask to have a picture taken with me. Such is life on the road.

Although totally different in terrain and style, both Rush Creek and the Geneva Golf Club had come highly recommended, so I was glad to have had the opportunity to play both courses.

While in Maple Grove, before and after playing Rush Creek, I stayed at the Hilton Garden Inn. This was the first time my accommodations had been arranged for me at one of Hilton's new concept hotels. It was well-decorated, clean, and comfortable with large bedrooms and suites, an indoor pool, a restaurant serving breakfasts and dinners, meeting rooms, and one of the things I was always thrilled to have: free in-room Wi-Fi. I hoped I would be given the opportunity to stay in other Garden Inns during my next four months.

Following golf and a wave good-bye to my new female Minnesota friends, I headed northwest again—this time to Fargo, North Dakota.

North Dakota – "Warm in Fargo"

During my two-hour drive from Alexandria, Minnesota to Fargo, I reflected on all that I knew about Fargo. I realized my knowledge was very limited. All I knew was what I had seen in the movie, *Fargo*, and from my brief discussions with Bob and Terri Johnston, good friends in California who were from North Dakota. I did know that, in the winter, it was very cold, and that Fargo—which was named after William Fargo, who founded Wells Fargo Express—got lots of snow and more than its share of flooding during and following heavy rain and snowy winters. I was pleased I was arriving on August 18 and wasn't going to have to be concerned about cold, snow, or flooding. As it turned out, the weather was quite nice, warm but not excessively hot.

After crossing the Red River and the border at Moorhead, Minnesota, I drove straight to the 310-room Holiday Inn, where I would stay for three nights thanks to the Fargo-Moorhead CVB. The hotel, which at the time was the state's largest, was well-situated for me. It was close to the two golf courses I would play, across the street from the Roger Maris museum I would visit, and close to the Newman Outdoor Field baseball stadium where I was scheduled to attend a minor league game between the Fargo–Moorhead Red Hawks and the Rockland Boulders. (I loved going to minor league games. I have always been intrigued by the names of minor league teams).

Besides the excellent restaurant, where I had breakfast each morning, and my spacious and comfortable room, where I spent down time on my computer, the Holiday Inn also had a large, indoor waterpark, which I enjoyed, and a self-service laundry where I washed my dirty clothes. Washing and drying my clothes in large washing machines and dryers was preferable to my usual way of washing clothes in the sink and then hanging them all over the room, hoping they would dry within a day or so.

My first day in Fargo was spent catching up on itinerary scheduling while my clothes were washing and drying. When they were dry, folded, and repacked in my suitcase, I walked across the street to the mall—not for shopping, though, as spending on non-essentials was out of the question. I went there to visit the Roger Maris Museum in the mall. Maris was born and raised in Fargo and played with the Red Hawks before becoming a star with the New York Yankees. Seeing his memorabilia, reading his statistics as a both a minor leaguer and a big leaguer, as well as learning about his life, was fascinating.

During my first day in Fargo, I also took time out to go to the aforementioned Red Hawks ball game. There, I not only enjoyed the game sitting in the great second-row seat provided me, but also took time to visit the Maury Wills Museum at the stadium. Although much smaller than Maris' museum, it was also extremely interesting. I was surprised to learn that, following his days as a base stealing All-Star shortstop with the Los Angeles Dodgers, Wills served for a short time as both a coach and an announcer for the Red Hawks.

My one day of golf in Fargo consisted of thirty-six holes. I teed off at 8:30 at the Edgewood Municipal Golf Course and at 4:30 at the Rose Creek Golf Course, two of the five public courses in Fargo run by the Fargo Park District. Edgewood and Rose Creek were quite different from each other. Edgewood was a Par 71 parkland course with trees lining the fairways, while Rose Creek was a wide-open Par 71 links-style course. Both were flat, as was the terrain in the valley, and both had plenty of water: nine holes where water came into play on Edgewood and thirteen holes at Rose Creek.

One of my favorite holes at Edgewood, which was established in the mid-1920s, was the Par 3 12th hole which was only 127 yards from the Whites. Although it was the eighteenth handicapped hole, it was still challenging. In order to hit the green, my tee shot had to fly over a field of deep, native grasses, which ran almost from tee to green, and it had to avoid a bunker strategically placed directly in front of the green. Fortunately, I hit a high eight-iron shot that avoided the hazards and stopped on the back edge of the green. I two-putted and walked away with a par, thus making it one of my favorite holes.

Following my round at Edgewood, where I shot 83, I drove three miles to visit the North Dakota State University campus and then made a quick trip back to the Holiday Inn to check for emails. I was expecting confirmations for accommodations and golf in upcoming states. During my years in sales and marketing, I prided myself on fast responses to phone calls and later to emails. I continued this approach during my year on the road. Doing so helped my credibility, which was essential when asking CVBs, PR agencies, B&Bs, hotels, motels, and golf courses to assist me with complimentary accommodations and golf.

After checking and responding to three important emails regarding future accommodations and golf, I drove to Rose Creek for my 4:30 tee time. I played from the Whites at 6,100 yards and, despite the fact that there was water on thirteen holes, I only had to reload once when my tee shot decided to "swim with the fishes." Despite my errant water ball, I was pleased with my score of 79, which turned out to be one of my better scores during the year.

The next day, before leaving Fargo for Sioux Falls, South Dakota, I lunched with Charley Johnson, president and CEO of the Fargo-Moorhead Conventions and Visitors Bureau. We ate at one of Fargo's "in spots," the HoDo restaurant in the landmark and newly renovated Hotel Donaldson on Broadway, Fargo's main street. While we enjoyed our delicious salads full of locally and organically grown fresh vegetables, Charley gave me great insight into Fargo's history and the surrounding countryside. Spending time with Charley was both interesting and educational.

When I left Fargo, I had a much greater understanding about the city—certainly much better than I did while driving in from Alexandria.

WEEK 38 – AUGUST 2

South Dakota – "Sioux Falls and Monuments"

In 1979, I was working as a sales representative with a foodservice brokerage company in the San Francisco Bay Area. I was asked to co-found a foodservice brokerage company by Ken Burk and Roy Scialabba, two salesmen who had been successful with another brokerage company. After much discussion and thought, I agreed, and we became partners in a new company: Northern California Food Sales. The name was chosen because it told where we were and what we did.

Over the years, besides sales and marketing, one of my duties was to organize, manage, and work show booths at distributor trade shows for the manufacturers we represented. Arranging for the electrical equipment, brochures, and food samples we needed for the shows wasn't hard physical work, but it took a great deal of organizing. At many of the five to ten shows we did a year, we would set up as many as twenty booths and have as many as forty employees preparing, demonstrating and selling products to the hundreds, and sometimes thousands, of customers who attended the shows.

I mention all the above because, driving to Sioux Falls, South Dakota from Fargo, I happily realized that at the three-day Travel Media Showcase I was about to attend—and during the three days following, when I would hit the links at two different golf courses—I wasn't going to have any responsibilities other than to listen, learn, and enjoy myself. I had been told by other travel writers I met who had attended previous TMS conferences that, before my two days of golf, I was going to be busy, busy, busy participating in the various meetings, tours, and events planned for us.

The Travel Media Showcase, an annual travel and tourism conference produced since 2000 by JoAnn Vero and her company, J. Vero & Associates, had been hosted yearly in different cities by Convention and Visitors Bureaus across the U.S. When I learned that TMS, as it is known, was to be held in Sioux Falls, South Dakota, I arranged my golf odyssey travel schedule so I could attend. The three days at TMS were extremely well organized by J. Vero & Associates and by Cathy Buchheim and her staff at the Sioux Falls CVB. We had thirty, fifteen-minute, one-on-one sessions where travel writers and media people met with CVB personnel. Along with writers and media from all over the U.S., I met with CVB representatives to learn about their cities and to develop contacts for future familiarization trips and articles.

We held each day's formal, one-on-one meetings in the Exhibit Hall in the Ramkota Hotel where the conference was being held. The Ramkota, one of Sioux Falls' largest and most well-known hotels, treated us really well. Both travel writers like myself and CVB attendees enjoyed excellent rooms as well as breakfasts, lunches, and dinners as part of TMS ... and once activities were through for the day, many of us relaxed in the hot tub or pool in the hotel's indoor water park.

After arriving in Sioux Falls and checking in for the three days of meetings and events, I joined a media tour group to take in the sights in and around Sioux Falls. Trying to review in detail everything we saw and all the activities that had been arranged for us could make for a book by itself. We were kept busy!

Here is a quick overview of what we did as attendees at TMS. We took tours of a number of Sioux Falls' museums and attractions, including the Pettigrew house, home and museum of South Dakota's first full-term senator. We toured the Washington Pavilion of Arts and Science, which housed a Performing Arts Center, a Science Discovery Center, a Visual Arts Center, a Community Learning Center, and the

Wells Fargo CineDome, which had a four-story-tall, domed screen that was sixty feet in diameter and weighed more than three tons.

We also toured the magnificently renovated ninety-seven-year-old Cathedral of Saint Joseph, which had just undergone a two-year restoration project. I was blown away when I looked at and touched the new marble columns. Not only were they gorgeous and smooth as could be, but they weren't marble! When I was told they were plaster with a faux finish made to look like marble, I was absolutely amazed. I would have lost money betting they were marble. We also attended a reception at Sanford Health, where we toured a new and very large, ultra-modern lab dedicated to diabetes, cancer, and children's rare diseases research.

Other tours included a visit to the Great Falls Zoo, to view some of the zoo's 1,000 animals from six continents, and to its adjacent Delbridge Museum of Natural History, which had an impressive collection of more than 150 mounted animals. We also attended a professional rodeo at the McCrossan Boys Ranch and enjoyed a Bar-B-Q at the Sioux Falls Outdoor Campus, which offers free outdoor adventures for both children and adults. We had a chance to further our knowledge about Sioux Falls with a tour of the Courthouse Museum, a restored 1800s courthouse filled with regional history exhibits.

I also joined a group of writers who toured a prehistoric Indian village and the Dakota Discovery Museum in Mitchell, seventy-five miles west of Sioux Falls. There, we also toured the world-famous Corn Palace, the multi-purpose arena/facility famous for its exterior walls decorated with large murals made of corn and grains. Our guide explained that roughly 275,000 ears of corn and 3,000 bushels of rye and other grains were used annually to make the murals, which are changed to a new theme every year. We were told that, to make the murals, the ears of corn were sawed in half lengthwise and nailed to the building following patterns created by local artists. They were spectacular and like nothing I had ever seen or could have ever imagined.

Following our Mitchell tours, we visited the small town of Freeman near Mitchell. We walked through the Prairie Arboretum, toured the Heritage Hall Museum, and drove a few miles to visit, through special, pre-arranged permission, a Hutterite Colony, home to a religious sect which traced its roots back to the Radical Reformation in the 16th century.

Following the three days of TMS, I played golf at Prairie Green and Elmwood, the top two public courses in the region. Prairie Green and Elmwood were, like Edgewood and Rose Creek in North Dakota, totally different courses. Prairie Green was a links-style course with wide, flat fairways and marshes that came into play. Elmwood was a parkland course full of trees where more precise shots were needed to hit somewhat narrower fairways. Playing from the Whites, from about 6,100 yards at both courses, was a good challenge to my "middle of the road" golfing skills.

If you have gotten the notion that my six days in Sioux Falls were busy, you are definitely correct. Up early and late to bed, every waking minute was educational and enjoyable. The one-on-one meetings with CVB representatives at the Travel Media Showcase helped me develop contacts for additional future accommodations and travel articles. Gaining insight into the myriad of activities available to Sioux Falls residents and visitors was invaluable. And ... playing golf at Edgewood and Rose Creek was relaxing, fun, and very enjoyable. I was sorry when my time in Sioux Falls came to an end. However, my adventures in South Dakota were hardly over.

After leaving Sioux Falls, I drove west to my next destination, the Custer State Park Game Lodge near Rapid City. On my way, I stopped at the Wall Drug Store in the small town of Wall on Highway 90, only a few miles east of Rapid City. I just had to see what Wall Drug was all about. For miles and miles, I had been seeing Burma Shave-type signs enticing me to stop for a free drink of ice-cold water. Ted and Dorothy Hustead began this marketing concept to draw thirsty travelers to their store shortly after they purchased Wall Drug in 1931. The concept worked. Wall Drug had grown and expanded from the original small store to encompass a number of buildings. It is known to attract upwards of 20,000 visitors a day during the summer months, most of whom, I imagine, buy something—because browsing through Wall Drug was like visiting a combination eclectic gift store, restaurant, and ice cream parlor that was full of memorabilia everywhere I looked. Even for a non-shopper like myself, it was a marvelous place to visit.

After Wall, I drove through portions of the Badlands National Park and the Black Hills National Park on my way to my next accommodations at the Custer State Park Game Lodge. Just before I reached the lodge, I was welcomed by a herd of forty to fifty buffalo that stood in the road close to my car. I could have rolled down my window and touched the huge one standing next to my car. Since it was possible one of the calves next to this wooly creature might have been its calf, I decided that exciting this mammoth animal by honking my horn in an effort to get it and the herd off the roadway wouldn't be a good idea. Fortunately, because I was in my car, the buffalo didn't seem to be as concerned about me as I was concerned about it and the herd. Finally, after the herd sauntered on to the nearby pasture, I was able to proceed and register at the lodge.

Once settled in my rustic but very comfortable cabin, I planned my next day's visits to Mount Rushmore to view the faces of Presidents George Washington, Thomas Jefferson, Teddy Roosevelt, and Abraham Lincoln, and to view the construction going on nearby at the Crazy Horse Memorial, the world's largest mountain carving. An immense project begun by sculptor Korczak Ziolkowski as a tribute to Native Americans, sculpting the mountain had been going on for more than sixty-four years. Based upon what I heard, it could take as long as another fifty to seventy-five years to complete.

From day one, Ziolkowski was a strong believer in the free enterprise system. He felt the Crazy Horse Monument should be built by interested people and not by the taxpayers. Since his death in 1982, his family has continued his work and his philosophy by continually refusing government funds, which could certainly speed up work on the project. Ziolkowski knew the project was larger than any one person's lifetime, so he left detailed plans to be used, along with scale models. When completed, the monument will be the world's largest mountain carving. It will be 563 feet high and 641 feet long. To give those numbers prospective, the faces on Mount Rushmore are 60 feet high.

Following this busy, busy week in South Dakota, I packed my suitcase, thanked my hosts at the lodge, and headed for my next destination: the Cornhusker State of Nebraska.

WEEK 39 – AUGUST 29

Nebraska – "A Course Named Horse"

After finishing my busy week in South Dakota, I drove southwest from the Rapid City area to the Prairie Club in Nebraska which was located just a few miles south of the South Dakota border. Thanks to Shannon Peterson, the Media Relations Coordinator for the Nebraska Department of Economic Development, and Kyle Schock, the Marketing and Sales Associate at the Prairie Club, I had been invited to stay at the resort and play the semi-private club's two championship courses, The Dunes and The Pines.

Both the Dunes, designed by Tom Lehman and Chris Brand, and the Pines, designed by Graham Marsh, were Par 73 beauties rather unique in design. Neither had water hazards or out-of-bounds. However, the native prairie grasses;

the numerous fairway, greenside, and waste bunkers; and the very fast, multi-tiered greens, which had huge breaks and were stimped at 12 when I played, gave me plenty to think about.

My favorite hole on the two courses was the Par 3 16th hole on the Dunes, as it had one of the best views of the sweeping prairies on the golf course. It could be played from 118 to 201 yards, and the green was a long, long thing of beauty. I was so taken back by the size of the green that I paced it off. It was ninety-one yards long and had a three- or four-foot-deep swale along one side of a portion of the green. Looking back, I now consider the green to have been the most memorable of the more than 2,500 greens I played during my golf odyssey.

Four suggestions if you ever get the opportunity to play the Prairie Club courses:

1. *Take a caddy or play with members who know the courses.* This will save you strokes, particularly on the greens … and you won't get lost. Since no one was scheduled to play the morning I was going to play the Pines, I was told the assistant pro would play with me, because otherwise, I would get lost. Lost? How could one ever get lost on a golf course? Once I played the course, I understood. There were significant distances between the greens and tees, and because of the desire to keep the courses "Pure Golf, the Way Golf Was Meant to be Played," as stated in the Prairie Club slogan, there were few directional signs.

2. *Play from the correct tees based on your handicap.* It is always tempting to play PGA Tour-length courses as the pros play them. However, unless you are a scratch or very low handicapper, think twice about playing the courses from the tips … the Pines plays to 7,405 yards and the Dunes to 8,073 yards. There are five sets of tees on the Pines and six sets on the Dunes course. No matter which tees you choose, the courses will be challenging.

3. *Bring your best putting game. You'll need it.*

4. *Although you can buy more balls in the well-stocked pro shop,* you should think about bringing more balls than you normally use. Balls are easily lost in the thick Prairie grass. Trust me, I know this for a fact.

In addition to the Dunes and Pines courses, The Prairie Club had a unique third course, a ten-hole Par 3 course. It was unique in that any of its holes could be played from anywhere on the course. Players call their shots, similar to the way the game of Horse is played on the basketball court. The winner of the previous hole gets to choose the next hole, which can be played from any place, any stance, any distance, any lie, to any green on the course. What a great concept for fun and competition among golfing buddies.

If played from the designated tees, the course played from 724 to 939 yards with the average hole length of ninety-five yards. Since I was the only one on the course when I played, I had a chance to work on my short game. I would love to play the course again someday using the Horse concept. Playing with my golf buddies in that manner would be a great opportunity to verbally harass them. (Sorry ladies … it's a guy thing).

The club's Lodge was wonderful. My room was one of the thirty-one well-appointed rooms, with thick down comforters and plush pillows on a very comfortable bed. It also had a large leather chair to relax in while watching TV, and a spacious tiled shower for my early-morning showers before enjoying the club's bountiful complimentary buffet breakfast. In the evening, the room was a nice place to relax after golf prior to a drink in the club's bar before choosing between a casual meal and a fine-dining dinner in the restaurant.

It was easy to feel truly relaxed in the Lodge's quiet, prairie surroundings. After my three days at the Prairie Club, I understood why it was selected by *Golfweek* as "One of the Top 25 Golf Resorts in the U.S." in its November, 2010 issue and why *Golf Digest* in December, 2010 named it "The Best Overnight Golf Destination."

I thought the Prairie Club's two links courses, with no water and no OB, were as close as you could come to playing Scottish and Irish links-style courses without venturing across the pond. If you are holding back on a golfing vacation in Scotland or Ireland because of the cost of the air fare, consider a golf vacation and/or membership at the Prairie Club in the Sand Hills Region of Nebraska. You will be able to eliminate long flights and still enjoy links-style golf as played in Scotland and Ireland.

Colorado – "The Broadmoor and Pike's Peak"

A number of years ago my second wife, Dianne, and I had the opportunity to spend time at the Broadmoor Hotel in Colorado Springs. I was there representing my company at a national sales meeting of the J.M. Smucker company, the jam and jelly company with what I have always thought was a great slogan: *"With a name like Smucker's, it has to be good."*

Remembering the fabulous time we had enjoying the Broadmoor Resort and its golf courses, I was quite pleased to be able to schedule another visit to Colorado Springs while on my tour and to have the opportunity to play two of the Broadmoor Golf Club's three courses, The East Course and the Mountain Course.

The Broadmoor, a destination resort for nearly one hundred years, opened in 1918. But its history dates all the way back to 1880, when it was known as the Broadmoor Dairy Farm. In 1890, Prussian Count James Pourtales purchased the land and ran a small dairy farm on the property. When he realized the dairy farm wouldn't make a good return on his investment, he decided to make an upper-class suburb of Colorado Springs with amenities which would increase the value of home sites. He formed the Broadmoor Land Investment Company and purchased the original 2,400 acre tract. Because he was interested in selling lots, he built the Broadmoor casino, which he opened July 1, 1891, and a few years later built The Broadmoor Hotel.

On May 9, 1916, Spencer Penrose, a Philadelphia entrepreneur who had made his fortune in gold and copper mining, purchased the Broadmoor casino and the hotel's forty-acre site and an adjoining 400 acres. He was desirous of turning the Pike's Peak region into the most interesting, multifaceted resort in the area and he had the money to do it. The Broadmoor Hotel expanded over the years, and when I was there in 2012, had 744 suites, rooms, and cottages, all excellent and luxuriously appointed.

Having spent a number of years of my business career calling on restaurants, hotels, colleges, etc. etc., an amazing fact about the Broadmoor jumped out at me. Over the years, the Broadmoor had had only six presidents and four executive chefs. This is pretty much an unheard of statistic in the hospitality industry, and certainly a testament to the "quality of life" at the resort.

While in Colorado Springs, I stayed with my cousin, Jim Ondler, and his wife, Rosalyn, at their home, located a few blocks above the Broadmoor. From their home, from the golf courses, and from The Broadmoor, I could hear the lovely sounds of the carillon bells at the Will Roger shrine, located in the Cheyenne Mountains that overlook Colorado Springs and the enormous valley in which the city resides. Every quarter hour during the day, the bells rang Westminster Chimes which could be heard as many as twenty miles away.

Listening to the bells every quarter hour while playing golf was quite something. They were loud but peaceful. I thought they might interfere with my golf game, but actually, they had the opposite effect. During my rounds on the East and Mountain Courses, the chimes made me relax and enjoy my surroundings. They were actually quite soothing.

The East Course, when it was completed in 1918, was the highest golf course in the world at 6,500 feet in elevation. I learned it is now a combination of holes originally designed by Donald Ross mixed in with holes by Robert Trent Jones, Sr. The course has quite a history, having been the site of five NCAA Championships and numerous PGA, LPGA, and Champions Tour Majors. Jack Nicklaus won his first major, the US Amateur, there in 1959. Annika Sorenstam won the US Women's Open there in 1995, and Eduardo Romero won the US Senior Open there in 2008.

From the Whites at 6,657 yards, it was longer than I was accustomed to playing. However, I happily found my shots went farther due to its 6,500 foot elevation, which to some degree overcame the additional yardage. The East Course was a fun course to play as its relatively wide fairways suited my "spray game." It had towering trees lining the fairways. Fortunately, I managed to avoid them most of the time—the key phrase being "most of the time." It also had large greens with more false fronts than a foursome of Hollywood starlets.

Following a great day of golf on the East Course, Rosalyn joined Jim and me in the Summit, one of the resorts eight locations for drinks and/or dining. We enjoyed a drink and then they gave me a quick tour of the hotel. We wandered throughout the hotel's shops, lounges, conference and meeting room facilities, and its numerous cafes and casual and white-table-cloth restaurants.

Following our tour, I told Jim and Rosalyn I thought it would be safe to say that once you check into the Broadmoor, with all of its wonderful facilities—including its services and recreational activities—you would never have to leave the premises.

The second course I played, the Mountain Course, had big greens that looked pretty benign but definitely were not. I learned the importance of staying below the hole when the speed and slope of the greens turned a couple of my downhill, ten-foot putts into twenty footers coming back.

The Par 72 course played to 7,700 yards from the tips. I can't imagine playing it from that length, particularly in the robust wind that Jim and I played in.

A reconfiguration by the Nicklaus Design Group of the original Arnold Palmer design, the Mountain Course is generally thought to be the most challenging of the Broadmoor's three courses. Both Jim and I understood why after completing our round fighting the wind, the dramatic elevation changes, the hilly, sloping fairways, and the many long carries over natural hazards. It was a tough course, but we enjoyed our day playing it, even with its many challenges.

The Mountain Course, like the East Course, also had numerous false fronts and deep bunkers—and a few medium-sized greens on which it appeared elephants had been buried. It had wide fairways, large, undulating greens, and magnificent views from many of the tees and greens. These views made me think I was in an IMAX theater with a full 360-degree view of the Cheyenne Mountains that towered above the course, the vast valley below, and the city of Colorado Springs.

While in Colorado Springs, in between golf on the East Course and the Mountain Course, I visited the Air Force Academy and its stunning chapels as well as the Garden of the Gods Park, where I viewed fascinating sandstone rock structures. I rode the Pike's Peak Cog Railway to the 14,115-foot summit. The bright red cog rail car, which held

218 passengers, took me on a slow but steady 8.9-mile route through four life zones, past cascading streams, gigantic boulders and tall pines and from lush, high plains to fragile, alpine tundra.

My cog railway journey started at the historic Manitou Springs Depot, where I boarded the train for an incredible journey on the world's highest cog railway. I was amazed when the rail car conductor explained the Pike's Peak Cog Railway had been entertaining visitors since 1891. Building it through canyons and up the steep Pike's Peak grade to reach the 14,115-foot summit must have been an almost-impossible task. When we reached the summit, the conductor explained that, in 1893, the scenic grandeur inspired a passenger, Katherine Lee Bates, to write a poem which later became a song we know and love: "America the Beautiful."

On September 5, after golf on the Mountain Course, I completed my visit to Colorado Springs with a sincere desire to return to enjoy the luxury of the hotel and the spectacular golf courses. I would have loved to have stayed longer, but I had to leave to prepare to fly to Reno, Nevada for a few days before flying on to my next state: Alaska.

I drove to Denver, where I stayed overnight with a Delta Upsilon fraternity brother, Jim Burton and his family. Jim, who was a DU at San Jose State long after I had graduated, had emailed me a few months earlier with an offer of accommodations when he read about my golf odyssey in the DU Quarterly, our fraternity's national publication. Jim and his family's gracious hospitality included overnight accommodations and the opportunity to park my car at their home for thirteen days while in Reno and Alaska. It also gave Jim and me a chance to reminisce about our DU days. Their hospitality was wonderful and it helped me save a considerable amount of money, which I greatly appreciated.

WEEK 41 – SEPTEMBER 10

Alaska – "Lucky with My Timing"

Having been to Anchorage once before while on an Alaskan cruise and land tour, I was looking forward to another visit to Alaska's most populous city, a cosmopolitan city of just under 300,000 inhabitants. On my previous visit I had found Anchorage to be a very friendly city with excellent restaurants, museums, and natural beauty. My one concern, as I planned my visit, was the weather. I recalled that September weather in Anchorage could be all over the ballpark. Since I had been rained on only four or five times in my previous eight months on the road, I dreaded the thought of having to don my rain gear to play golf in the rain or a light snow.

I was lucky with the timing of my visit. The week before I flew in from Reno, a freak storm swept across the area

242

with 100-mile-per-hour winds, and the week after I was there a ferocious rainstorm brought about massive flooding, which closed the courses I played. During my six-day stay in our forty-ninth state, it was chilly but the sun shone. I was definitely lucky with my timing.

I played two military courses open to the public while in Anchorage, Eagleglen, located on the Joint Base Elmendorf-Richardson military base, and the Creek Course, one of the two nearby Moose Run military-managed courses. Eagleglen and the Creek Course were in pretty good shape, considering the freak windstorm the week before I played them had knocked down hundreds of trees on both courses.

Eagleglen, designed by Robert Trent Jones, Jr. and named in past years as "Best in Alaska" by *Golf Digest*, and the Creek Course at Moose Run, thought to be the most difficult course in Alaska, were flat with average to wide fairways, thick forests on the fairway perimeters, and ponds and creeks to avoid when hitting fairway shots. A number of fairways still had fallen trees scattered about as a result of the storm the week before. As a result, both courses had instituted a local rule that allowed me a free drop from the fallen trees.

Although I only saw one fox while playing, I was told following my rounds that deer, moose, and an occasional bear were sometime seen on the courses. I'm glad I was told this after my rounds. Deer I could have handled, but moose and bear … no thanks. (Due to dwindling golf revenue and increased costs, Eagleglen was closed by the military in 2014).

While in Anchorage, I stayed at the Clarion Suites Hotel. My suite was both spacious and comfortable, the staff was extremely helpful, and the hotel was well equipped with a fitness center, an indoor pool and spa, and free Wi-Fi. I took advantage of the complimentary buffet breakfasts and free airport shuttle. This allowed me to save some of the money I had won by playing penny slots during my three days in Reno prior to flying to Anchorage. I had lost my $20 daily gambling limit each of the first two days I was there, but on the third day prior to my flight to Anchorage, I hit four threes on a video poker game, won $138, and immediately pocketed my money and headed to the bar for a celebratory drink.

The Clarion was just a ten-minute walk to Anchorage's main downtown area, which was a hub for restaurants, museums, and shopping. (I only know about shopping because on my previous visit, my wife and I wandered into a number of stores, including the upscale Nordstrom department store). Nordies in Alaska … who would have thought?

One day while not golfing, catching up on emails and/or working on my radio segment, I boarded the Red Trolley for a one-hour informative tour of Anchorage, which included a drive by Lake Hood (the largest and busiest float-plane base in the world, and Cook Inlet, where the tides are the second largest in the world). I also took time out to tour the very interesting and educational Anchorage Museum of History and Art. I finished the day by walking about downtown, asking local residents about the city, and having dinner at the Glacier Brew House, Alaska's number one brewpub and one of Anchorage's top restaurants.

Having eaten a marvelous dinner there on my previous visit, I decided to dine there again in spite of the dent it would make in my daily food budget. Fortunately I was able to negotiate a complimentary dinner in return for a mention on my *Real Golf Radio* segment. I immersed myself in the fun atmosphere of the restaurant, watched couples and families enjoying a night out, and thoroughly enjoyed my dinner, which included two delicious house specialties, a herb-crusted halibut entrée, and a crème brulee dessert. Dining at the white table cloth Glacier Brew House was quite a treat. The ambience, food, and very professional waiters and waitresses reminded me of some of the casual yet sophisticated restaurants I had eaten in while living in the San Francisco Bay Area.

My final day in Anchorage was a catch-up day before heading to the airport for my 8:30 PM red-eye flight to Reno via Dallas. It was to be a long flight with a lengthy layover in Dallas, but I was excited about it as I was on my way to play golf with buddies in the twenty-fifth annual version of the almost world famous Fagapo Invitational Golf Tournament.

Alaska is a gorgeous state with beautiful scenery, excellent fishing, and friendly people. If you haven't been to our forty-ninth state, put a trip there on your Bucket List, and be sure to include a visit to Anchorage. You will be glad you did. One suggestion: If you fly to Anchorage, plan a daytime flight. You'll see spectacular snowcapped mountaintops, massive glaciers inching their way toward lakes and bays, and possibly get a view of Mt. McKinley, the highest mountain peak in the U.S.

WEEK 42 – SEPTEMBER 16

California – "FAGAPO Means Camaraderie"

Months before my arrival in Colorado, I organized my schedule to fly to Reno for a few days of R & R following golf in Colorado and prior to flying to Alaska, my forty-first state. I also organized a return to Reno and a quick drive to California to play my twenty-fifth year in the almost-world-famous FAGAPO Invitational Golf Tournament.

In 1987, I, along with Dan Cochrane, a good friend and neighbor in Walnut Creek, California, were members of the Oak Grove Swim and Tennis Club, a small neighborhood club. Once a month, as many as fifteen or twenty fellow tennis players gathered at the club for a round-robin tennis tournament. Dan and I were the only members of the group who played golf on a somewhat regular basis, although some had played occasionally over the years. We suggested to the group that it would be fun to have a one-day men's golf and tennis getaway at Lake Tahoe, some four hours away. The idea was well-received.

Nine of us gathered a few months later and packed our clubs, some of which had to be borrowed. We gathered up a couple of decks of cards, a box of old poker chips, and our tennis rackets and drove to Lake Tahoe for a one-day men's golf and tennis get-away. Needing a name for our outing, we came up with FAGAPO, an acronym which stood for First Annual Golf and Poker Outing.

FAGAPO expanded over the years from its humble beginning to become a much-anticipated, four-day, four-night outing. Twenty-four golfers now play on three excellent courses in and around the small hamlet of Graeagle, forty-five minutes north of Lake Tahoe. Participants in the yearly tournament have graduated from the first year's bunk beds and old couches and now enjoy four-bedroom condos, dinners out, and all types of prizes for daily and overall winners. Players even have and wear three official FAGAPO golf shirts emblazoned with our FAGAPO Invitational logo.

I wasn't about to miss attending FAGAPO, as I had attended each of the previous twenty-four years. Following golf in Alaska, I flew from Anchorage to Reno via Dallas to stay, along with several other FAGAPO participants, at the Truckee, California home of fellow FAGAPO-ite Bob Johnson and his wife Elaine. You might ask why I would choose to fly such a circuitous route. The answer: when you use frequent flyer miles and that is all that is available, that's what you do.

Flying from Anchorage to Reno via Dallas had been a long trip. So, after a number of vodka screwdrivers, glasses of Merlot, and a delicious dinner at the Johnson's, I crashed. The next morning, I was up early, played a practice round with seven other FAGAPO-ites at Gray's Crossing—a splendid, Peter Jacobsen-designed course in Truckee—and then drove to Graeagle to begin FAGAPO 25.

We played FAGAPO 25 on three outstanding courses, all within twenty minutes of our five, four-bedroom condos at the Plumas Pines Golf Resort, which we rented through Ellen Cantrell of Plumas Pines Vacation Homes and Rentals. All three courses had "Kodak Moment" postcard scenery with groves of tall pines, colorful wildflowers, and sky-blue lakes and streams.

The first day, we played Whitehawk Ranch, a *Golfweek Magazine* award-winning course which had been carved through the natural terrain of a vast mountain valley. It featured fairways framed with native grasses and tall pines and seven streams that created ponds which added to the beauty and challenge of the course.

The second day, we played Grizzly Ranch in nearby Portola, an immaculately groomed private club which had been opened for public play. Surrounded by more than a million acres of pristine national and state forest lands, it was extremely scenic. It had numerous elevation changes and an abundance of lengthy uphill and downhill holes. The third and final day, we played the always-well-groomed Plumas Pines course. Although not a target course, it was definitely one where accurate shots were important because of its narrow fairways, tall pines, ball-swallowing small lakes and ponds, and left and right dog legs.

If you happen to be at Plumas Pines on a Thursday in late September, look for us. We'll be the ones wearing black golf shirts, sipping beers as we surround the 18th green awaiting the arrival of the tournament leaders playing their last hole. Join us for a beer as we anxiously await the outcome of the tournament.

After three days of golf on excellent courses, a wonderful dinner at the Whitehawk Lodge; pizza from Gumbas Pizza, now renamed Anton's Grille; and tri tips and salads catered by Longboards, Plumas Pines award winning restaurant—we doled out daily and overall prize money to our winners. Our FAGAPO 25 champion was "Bazooka" Jim Grove. Jim took home prize money, the FAGAPO winner's trophy, the FAGAPO Invitational Waterford Crystal Vase, a congratulatory letter signed by Jack Nicklaus and … the Coveted FAGAPO Blazer, a garish 1960's Nicklaus blazer which Dan Cochrane had donated many years before. We had sent the blazer to Nicklaus and asked if he would autograph it for us. He graciously did so and returned it, along with a signed congratulatory letter on his personal stationery.

We gave out tournament awards while enjoying our annual Awards Dinner at one of our favorite restaurants in the area, The Iron Door in nearby Johnsville. At the dinner, we also bowed our heads and honored the memory of Oscar Temple, "The Big O from Yazoo City," and two other FAGAPO-ites who had passed away over the years: Rich Cullen and Tom Yerkes. All three had been our good friends for years and years.

Because most of our FAGAPO participants were Medicare-eligible, during FAGAPO 25, neither the age of the participants nor their golf ability was important. What was important was that everyone enjoyed an outing with good friends. We laughed and told jokes as if we were kids again. We wished we could hit our tee shots 300-plus yards like the pros we watch on TV. We acted like winning the Coveted FAGAPO Blazer was as prestigious and financially rewarding as winning The Masters Green Jacket. What we didn't have to pretend was the enjoyment we had gathering to reminisce about family friendships and twenty-five years of FAGAPO. I wouldn't have missed it for anything.

Competing for the Coveted FAGAPO Blazer and enjoying FAGAPO camaraderie was a special treat. I was sorry when it was over, but I couldn't put my golf odyssey on hold. I flew back to Denver and, the next day, drove to my next state: Wyoming.

Wyoming – "Eight Foot Cowboy Boots"

A short hour-and-a-half drive from Denver and its sprawling, urban setting took me to Cheyenne, Wyoming's capital city with a somewhat rural population of about 60,000. Named a number of years back as the nation's No. 1 True Western Town, I found Cheyenne's history of cowboys, railroads, and "All Things Western" to be quite intriguing. I learned that, when the area was first settled, Cheyenne had become quite a railroad town—in fact, it was known as "America's Railroad Capital" as men moved west to work on the transcontinental railroad.

I had driven to Cheyenne for a short, three-day visit to absorb its Western background and culture and to play golf at two of the city's four public courses, the 18-hole Airport Golf

Club and the 9-hole Little America Course at Cheyenne's Little America Hotel and Resort, where I stayed. The Little America course, which surrounded the resort, was a Par 30 course with three Par 4s and six Par 3s. It played from 1,550 to 1,900 yards, had tree-lined fairways, and water that came into play on the first three holes. Although short in length, it had plenty of challenges. Its sloping fairways, water hazards, strategically placed bunkers, small greens, and tall trees which lined its fairways, made shot placement especially important. It was definitely not a "Kiss Your Sister" course, in spite of its short yardage.

The Airport Golf Club was a flat course with both easy and difficult dog legs. It was also a relatively short course, as it played to only 6,100 yards from the tips. It had two distinctly different nines. The front nine was narrow with lots of trees, while the back nine was wide open. While playing the Airport course, which was the home course for the Wyoming Open, Wyoming's only professional golf tournament, I enjoyed being paired with three local golfers who gave me insight into the course, its leagues, tournaments, and the Cheyenne area.

The Little America Resort where I stayed was Wyoming's premier location for weddings and conventions. It had 188 spacious, remodeled rooms, an outdoor Olympic-size swimming pool, an upscale dining room, and a casual café with gourmet coffees and pastries. It was a great place to relax after my hectic schedules in Colorado, Alaska, and California.

Cheyenne, home to the Cheyenne Frontier Days—the world's largest outdoor rodeo and Western celebration, with ten days of world-class rodeo action and Western entertainment—was a busy railroad and cowboy town as the U.S. was moving westward in the 1860s. As a result, there were many interesting museums in town devoted to the area's history. I visited three of them: the Cheyenne Train Depot Museum, which is a National Historic Landmark; the Nelson Museum of the West, which housed exhibits featuring native-American artifacts, cowboy trappings, 19th century weapons, and outlaw memorabilia; and the Cheyenne Frontier Days Old West Museum, which had Frontier Days memorabilia, vintage carriages, and rodeo exhibits.

I also took a fully narrated and extremely educational, ninety-minute tour of the city on the Cheyenne Street Railway Trolley. During the tour, I saw a number of the nineteen, eight-foot-tall, colorfully painted cowboy boots that are situated throughout town. The boots, painted by local artists to show not only Cheyenne's history but that of Wyoming as well, were very impressive. While on the trolley, I was also able to see "Big Boy," the world's largest steam locomotive, which I was told weighed in at 1,208,760 pounds. Built in 1941 for use by the Union Pacific Railroad on the steep grades from Cheyenne to Ogden, Utah, the locomotive was massive.

I also had time to wander through the very walkable downtown area. I picked up a free brochure at the Cheyenne

WYOMING – "EIGHT FOOT COWBOY BOOTS"

Depot, which is acknowledged as one of the most beautiful railroad stations in North America, and spent half a day on a self-guided walking tour of downtown visiting museums and checking out the local watering holes.

I learned a great deal about railroads and the Old West during my time in Cheyenne, as there was history galore to be seen and read about. For anyone intrigued by railroad history and/or the Old West, Cheyenne definitely deserves a visit. There's plenty to see and do for both young and old.

Following my quick three days in Cheyenne, I headed for Utah and a week's stay at my daughter and son-in-law's home in Sandy near Salt Lake City. I was going to "babysit" my granddaughter, Shanna, as my daughter Lisa and son-in-law Mike were going on vacation to Grand Cayman in the Caribbean. Since my granddaughter was a junior in high school, had her driver's license, and was not only a good student but a joy to be around, it was more like she was babysitting Grandpa.

I had a wonderful time visiting with Shanna. Every grandparent should have such an opportunity. I felt very fortunate my travel schedule allowed me to spend time with her before I had to hit the road again and traveled north to The Big Sky state of Montana.

Interesting trivia about Cheyenne:

- The telephone book's first yellow pages were printed there in 1881, when the local phone company ran out of white paper.

- Neil Diamond lived in Cheyenne as a child.
- Hollywood film stars Steve McQueen and Ali McGraw were married in Cheyenne's Holiday Park in 1973.
- United Airlines trained its stewardess in Cheyenne in the 1940s.
- Famed sports broadcaster Curt Gowdy lived in Cheyenne as a child. A park in the city is named after him.

Montana – "Black Sand and a Sly Fox"

Following a wonderful week in Utah with my grand-daughter Shanna, while my daughter and son-in-law were on vacation in Grand Cayman, I headed north for my visit to Montana. On my seven-hour, four-hundred-plus-mile drive to Butte, I crossed grassy prairies, viewed mountains rising high in the distance, and saw buffalo roaming in fenced-in pastures.

Although my route took me relatively close to Yellowstone National Park, I didn't have time to tour the park. I had been told a full day was absolutely necessary to drive though the park and get to see Old Faithful, the world's most famous geyser. Unfortunately, I couldn't spare that amount of time, as the Butte Convention and Visitors Bureau had arranged reservations for me at the Fairmont Hot Springs Resort near Butte. I was sorry I didn't have the opportunity to watch Old Faithful shoot a stream of thousands of gallons of boiling water up to 145 feet in the air. Sadly, I realized a visit to Yellowstone would have to remain on my "Bucket List."

When I checked in at the resort, described to me as "Montana's Premier Hot Springs Resort," I was quite pleased. In addition to my very comfortable room, the resort had indoor and outdoor spring-fed pools with 168-degree hot spring water cooled to comfortable temperatures; casual and fine dining, although my budget precluded the fine dining; and an eighteen-hole championship golf course. With these amenities—and a five-story, indoor water slide and a Putt-Putt Mini golf course, plus downhill and cross-country skiing nearby in the winter—I certainly understood why the resort was considered a favorite year-round destination.

The 6,741 yard Par 72 Fairmont Hot Springs Resort course, the first of the four courses I played in Montana, was enjoyable—even though it was only forty-one degrees when I teed off. Fortunately for this California wimp, I was provided with an enclosed golf cart, which helped me keep warm until the temperature rose to around sixty degrees. The course, like many I had played since leaving home in January, had wide, parallel fairways, well-placed bunkers, and ponds to be avoided. It was home to the longest hole in the state, the 649-yard Par 5 5th hole. The tee for number five was exactly one mile high at 5,280 feet above sea level. As a result of its elevation and the length of the hole, it was known as the "mile high, mile long" hole. Another interesting feature of the course was the third hole's three-tier, 10,000-square-foot green, the largest green in the state.

After two nights at the resort, which included times relaxing in the indoor/outdoor pool, I was up early for a short drive to Anaconda to play The Old Works, the Jack Nicklaus Signature Course managed by Troon Golf. Ground was broken in May of 1993 on what became a championship course, not only in length, but in challenges and conditions as well. Situated both on a valley floor and on severe sloping hills, it had numerous right and left dog legs and multiple elevation changes. It was well-known for its greenside bunkers and long fairway waste bunkers, which were filled with black sand, a by-product of copper smelting that once was the major industry in Anaconda.

Although water came into play on only four holes, the black sand bunkers, which were prevalent on almost every hole, gave the appearance of water. I was quite happy to have my stray shots land in the sand bunkers rather than in water. Although the black sand bunkers weren't necessarily easy to hit out of, at least I could find my stray shots. Playing from the 6,100 yard "Limestone" tees, I shot a rollercoaster 45-44 which included two 7's, two 8's and two birdies. Not good, not bad ... but a lot of fun.

After my round at The Old Works, I drove to Missoula, where I met my brother-in-law Chuck Stone, who had driven in from his family's vacation condo in Twin Lakes Village near Coeur d'Alene, Idaho. We were to play two rounds of golf together, as we had done many times during our fifty years of friendship dating back to our college days, mine at San Jose State and his at Santa Clara University.

We played Canyon River and The Ranch Club, which were just minutes from the Guest House Suites where we stayed. The hotel, which had eighty rooms and a large conference center, was conveniently located only minutes from both the University of Montana and downtown Missoula. To our surprise, the hotel had complimentary hot waffle breakfasts. The manager graciously comped not only my prearranged room but Chuck's as well. We greatly appreciated this gesture on her part.

Canyon River, which opened in 2006, was the first of the two courses Chuck and I played. It had been ranked #1 in the state and #9 in the nation for Courses Under $75. It was a public course with wide fairways, water on three holes, undulating greens, and a sly fox that stole golf balls. Although the fox didn't venture into our fairway to steal one of our golf balls, we did see it slinking about on an adjacent fairway, eyeing another foursome's little white dimpled spheres. Evidently, the fox was a well-known creature—not quite a pet, but definitely a favorite fixture.

Chuck and I had a fun day on the course reminiscing about our many years of friendship, how our families had all grown up, and how our grandchildren were almost the same age as we were when we first met. We laughed and had a great time. We had our usual $1 Nassau bet, and if my memory serves me correctly, Chuck took me for $2. I was glad to hand over the greenbacks because I remembered the golf bet slogan: "Fast Pay Means Fast Friends," and I wanted a chance the following day to recover my losses.

That night, we ate at a local hamburger hangout, downed a few brewskis, and continued to reminisce about the many funny times we had at the Millstone Meadows Invitational, a golf tournament we organized for a number of years when we both lived in the San Francisco Bay Area. We also thought of the sad times we had had over the years when friends and family members passed away. Mostly, we talked about how fortunate we were to be able to enjoy retirement after more than fifty years in the work force.

The following day, anxious to win back my two dollars, Chuck and I drove to The Ranch Club, a private course which was open for public play. It was a links-style course spread out over 343 acres of ranchland. While playing its well-manicured fairways and greens, it was easy to understand why it was highly rated by both *Golf Digest* and *Golfweek* magazines.

We loved the following comment on the back of its scorecard: "This is Montana. Not only does our rough live up to its name, but you may have to arm wrestle it to get your ball back." Playing from the 5,700 yard Silver Tees, we slugged it out with both good and bad shots. Happily for me, I played over my head and shot 39-38 with two birdies.

I won our $1 Nassau bet and came away one dollar ahead from our two days on two of Missoula's best courses. After the way I had played the day before, Chuck wanted me to take a urine test for steroids. Needless to say ... I declined.

The next day, when Chuck hit the road back to Twin Lakes, I toured the Missoula Smokejumper's Visitor Center. After reviewing the center's many displays, which explained fire-fighting procedures and smokejumping history, I watched several videos and entered an actual 1937 fire lookout. I got a real insight into the lives of the Missoula Smokejumpers, brave men and women who were charged with parachuting into wooded forests to provide the initial attack on small, emerging wilderness fires and to sustain suppression on larger fires. Coming away from the Visitor's Center, I was overwhelmed by the bravery of this contingent of men and women, who ranged in age from twenty to the early fifties, and by the training they had to go through to be certified as Missoula Smokejumpers.

Following my tour, I left for Twin Lakes, Idaho for a visit with Chuck and my sister-in-law, Ann, before heading on to Washington State. While driving into the mountains, I thought about what I had seen and experienced in Montana. I felt I had had a "Genuine Montana Experience," which was a slogan I had seen on a promotional piece about Montana.

Washington – "Only One Tree"

O ver the years, I had been to Seattle on five different occasions—so when planning my trip to the State of Washington, Seattle always came to mind. Now that I am home and writing about my time in Washington, I am reminded of Everett, Mukilteo, and University City, cities I visited while playing golf in the state named after our first President.

In addition to my two days of golf in Washington, I had very comfortable accommodations arranged for me in the cities of Everett and Mukilteo by Julie Gangler, the media relations representative for the Snohomish County Tourism Bureau. I stayed one night at the thirty-three-room boutique Inn at Port Gardner in Everett overlooking the Everett Marina, and two nights at the Staybridge Inn and Suites in

Mukilteo. Julie gave me an excellent overview of Snohomish County when we dined at Lombardi's Italian Restaurant next door to the Inn. Julie was extremely knowledgeable about the area and the fascinating and educational aviation-oriented tours she had scheduled for me.

The tours she had arranged included time at the Historic Flight Restoration Center in Mukilteo, where vintage aircraft produced between 1927 and 1957 were restored and displayed; walking through a working hangar which housed Microsoft co-founder Paul Allen's Flying Heritage Collection of 1935-1945 warbirds; touring Boeing's Future of Flight Aviation Center; and taking an amazing, ninety-minute walking tour of the Boeing plant, where their wide-body planes, including the then new 787 Dreamliner, were being assembled.

Just before I finished my Boeing tour, I was told one of the new Dreamliners was about to take off on a test flight from Boeing's adjacent airstrip. I, along with hundreds of other tourists and Boeing employees, watched the Dreamliner roar down the runway and glide effortlessly into the blue sky above. It was a sight to behold.

My two golf games in Washington were at Harbour Pointe Golf Club in Mukilteo, an hour north of Seattle, and at Chambers Bay in University Place, forty minutes south of Seattle. The front nine on Harbour Pointe, an Arthur Hills design, wound its way through a series of wetlands and featured water on all nine holes. The back nine was a totally different nine; it was played on rolling hills with evergreen trees lining the fairways. I loved Harbour Pointe's signature hole, the Par 4 11ᵗʰ because of its breathtaking view of Puget Sound. It was described to me as one of the most spectacular holes on the West Coast.

Before playing, when I asked the club's professional for a suggestion about how to play the course, he told me, "to score well, just hit to the 150-yard pole and you will be rewarded." I wish I had been able to follow his advice.

Chamber's Bay in University Place, just west of Tacoma, was my second course. Publicly owned by the city of University Place, it was to become world-famous as the host course of the 2015 US Open won by Jordan Speith. Voted "America's Best New Public Course for 2008" by *Golf Digest*, Chambers Bay was designed to challenge the greatest players in the world—and those of us who watched television coverage of the Open saw it did just that. When I played it, it was a course anyone could enjoy, as it played from 5,100 to 7,400 yards.

Even though there was only one tree on the course, and it didn't come into play, I considered Chambers Bay—which, like Harbour Pointe, was also located on Puget Sound—to be a target course. Tee shots and fairway shots had to be made to specific spots on the severe sloping fairways to set up second or third shots to well-guarded greens for potential birdies or pars.

Chambers Bay was a walking course with no golf carts allowed, so I walked up and down its hills, flailed away in its fescue rough, and shot a respectable 90 while my caddy, Nick, carried my clubs. If I hadn't had Nick as my caddy, I doubt if I would have broken 100. Nick had been at Chambers Bay since before it opened and knew the course like the back of his hand. He told me where to aim and how to approach the narrow entrances to the numerous bowl-shaped greens, and he advised me about the breaks in the greens, some of which were twenty feet or more. If you have the opportunity to play Chambers Bay, and Nick is still caddying there, ask for him to be your caddy. He is excellent.

My day playing Chambers Bay was made even more fun as I was able to invite my brother-in-law's son-in-law, Lance, and his son, Nick, (not the caddy) to play with me. Lance and my niece Tricia, son Nick, and daughter Natalie lived only two miles from the course. I stayed with them for three nights and thoroughly enjoyed the opportunity to hear about happenings in their lives. I even got to watch Nick, now a sophomore at Santa Clara University, play in a highly contested soccer game.

(Editor's note): When I saw Lance at a family reunion last year (in 2015), he related a story to me about one of his former summer school teachers, a sixth-grade math teacher. Lance, who was a school principal at the time and is now an Assistant Superintendent of Schools, was asked by the teacher if he could have an unpaid week off. He explained to Lance he had been asked by a young player to caddy in an upcoming golf tournament. After much consideration,

Lance approved the time off and his teacher caddied. This wouldn't be much of a story except the caddy's name was Michael Greller and the young player was Jordan Spieth. Greller's week off later became a year's sabbatical to caddy. Greller has now turned his love of golf and his golf prowess into a full-time, lucrative career touring the U.S. and the world as Spieth's caddy.

While in the Seattle area, I was also scheduled to play the Kayak Point Golf Course, thirty-five minutes north of Everett, but I lost my way while trying to find the course. I was just about to run out of gas when I spotted a gas station. It was closed, and as I learned later, had been out of business for a number of years. Since I was on a lightly used road, in a very rural location, in a heavily wooded forest with few street signs, and had no idea where another gas station was located, I began to think I might be spending the night in my car. Fortunately, a local resident drove by, and upon seeing my California license plate, stopped to ask if I was lost. When I explained my predicament, she offered to drive me to the one and only active gas station in the area. I thanked my lucky stars and hopped in her car. She drove me to the country store/gas station where I got a couple of gallons of gas. She then drove me back to my car, helped me add gas to my tank, and then guided me back to the gas station so I could fill up.

Realizing I was directionally challenged, since my GPS didn't work in the area, "my saving angel" offered to guide me to the golf course. She said she knew it well, as she played there often. When I arrived at the Kayak Point Golf Course, it was almost 4 p.m., two hours after my scheduled tee time. After explaining who I was and apologizing for any inconvenience I might have caused, I asked about the course. I was told it was carved from an old-growth forest of fir and cedar, had been selected previously as one of "America's Top Fifty Public Courses to Play" by *Golf Digest*, and had been recommended by the *Seattle Times* as a "Must Play" in the State of Washington. I am definitely going to play it when and I get back to the Seattle area ... but I'm going to make sure I have a full tank of gas and detailed directions as to how to get there.

Speaking of directions, I spent my last night in Washington programming my GPS to take me to Medford, Oregon in my forty-sixth state. I also set it up for a stop-over in Portland, where I was going to have lunch and a visit with my step-daughter, Kayla.

Oregon – "Largest Match-Play Venue"

A number of years ago, when I lived in Walnut Creek, California, several of my golf buddies and I drove to Medford, Oregon to play in a golf tournament. It wasn't just another tournament. It was the Southern Oregon Golf Championship Match-Play Tournament, the largest Amateur Match-Play Tournament in the United States held on a single course.

Competed at Medford's Rogue Valley Country Club—every year but one since 1929—416 men, women, senior and junior golfers teed-it-up on the twenty-seven-hole parkland course.

In the three years I participated in the tournament, I won my flight twice and was runner up once. It wasn't by consistently hitting the fairways. I was then, and am now, a scrambler. In the tournaments, I made shots through trees, out of the rough, and from behind ponds, that would have made Seve Ballesteros proud. I was also able to sink a number of long, curling putts that had my opponents scratching their heads. My buddies said my unorthodox winning shots proved that in golf at our level, "It's better to be lucky than good."

In setting up my itinerary and my visit to Oregon, I mapped out plans to revisit and play RVCC. Although I wasn't going to be there for the weeklong match-play festivities, which conclude each year on Labor Day, I wanted to once again play the course. I wanted to see if I could hit more of its flat and rolling, tree-lined fairways in regulation than I had when playing the tournaments. When I played it, I was both lucky and good. I hit more fairways and was pleased with my round of 86. I could only wish that it had been in the 2012 Match-Play Tournament.

I also played Centennial Golf Club, which was designed by two-time PGA Tour winner and 1977 US Amateur Champion John Fought. Fought, a native Oregonian, co-designed Pumpkin Ridge's Witch Hollow, where Tiger Woods won his third straight US Amateur title. When he designed Centennial, Fought turned a former historic pear orchard into a spectacular links-style course.

Before I teed off, I asked which of the five sets of tees would be best for a short-hitting twelve-handicapper like myself. I was told I could probably manage any of the tees, even the 7,309-yard Black Tees, which carried a course rating of 136. I remember saying, "Thanks for the confidence, but I would like to break 100." Since I had been playing tees from 5,500 to 6,100 yards, I settled on the Green Tees at 5,760 yards. After completing my round, I realized I had made a good decision. My 84 was right on the money, twelve strokes over par.

Opened in 1996, the Par 72 Centennial course was walkable, although I chose to ride, as it did have a few elevation changes. With water on six holes and wide fairways leading to well-guarded bentgrass greens, it was a marvelous course with great vistas of the valley and the Siskiyou Mountains. It was easy to understand why University of Oregon and Oregon State University alums chose it to be the site that year of their annual "Civil War Golf Tournament."

Thanks to the Travel Medford tourism group, while I was in Medford I had the opportunity to visit, tour, and sample treats on an hour-long tour of Harry and David's world-famous fruit and gift basket company. I watched cakes, cookies, and chocolates being made and saw how gift boxes and baskets full of delicious fruit were hand-packed, stacked, and shipped to all fifty states and 102 countries around the world. I also toured two locally owned and operated businesses: the eighty year-old Rogue Creamery Cheese Shop and Lillie Belle Farms, one of America's Top Ten Chocolatiers.

The Rogue Creamery Cheese Shop and the Lillie Belle Farms chocolate shop both carried a large variety of products. The Cheese Shop had over one hundred cheeses, including nine hand-crafted varieties of their own blue cheese. Lillie Belle Farms had over one hundred varieties of their hand-made chocolates. After sampling items at their locations, I understood why it had been suggested to me that I visit these two factory stores.

For a number of years, I lived forty-five minutes from California's Napa Valley and had the opportunity to do wine tastings at most of the Napa Valley wineries. When I was in Medford, I looked forward to tasting the local wines from the Applegate, Rogue, and Umpqua valleys. I wasn't disappointed.

I visited and had complimentary wine tastings at the RoxyAnn Winery near Rogue Valley Country Club and at the 2 Hawk Winery's newly constructed "Urban Farm Style" tasting room and restaurant across the street from the Centennial golf course. I also sampled wine at Ledger David winery's Le Petit Tasting Room, located conveniently between the Rogue Creamery Cheese Shop and the Lillie Belle Farms chocolate factory. Although I enjoy wine, I can't be considered as someone who is knowledgeable about the various idiosyncrasies of different wines. I didn't know how to rate the Oregon wines I was served except to say that, to my taste, they all deserved high praise.

Each day following golfing, touring, and/or wine tasting, I eagerly headed back to my comfortable suite at the

Homewood Suites to work on plans for visits to my final three states: Nevada, Utah, and Hawaii. While setting up my final schedules, I began to realize I was actually going to reach my goal of playing golf in all fifty states in fifty weeks. It was quite a feeling.

California – "Driving and Visiting"

The forty-seventh week of my journey was a totally different week for me. Actually, it really wasn't a week—it was a week and a half, as I wasn't scheduled to be in Las Vegas until the eighth of November. So, after leaving Medford, Oregon, I made the most of the opportunity. I spent my time driving from city to city in California, visiting friends and relatives.

I won't bore you with all the daily details of my eleven days of semi-leisure, which included only one round of golf, a fun round with buddies at Shadowridge Country Club, my former club in Vista, California. I will tell you it was a wonderful eleven days of seeing and hugging family members, relatives, old friends, and former business associates. It brought home to me once again how important it is to have a loving family and good friends.

Nevada/Utah – "Scenic Desert Views"

As a golf and travel writer, I have been fortunate to have been able to travel to, visit, and write about domestic and international locations and golf courses. In 2009, I joined nearly one hundred other golf writers and broadcasters and attended the 10th Annual Golf Media Classic held in Scottsdale, Arizona. Organized by Arizona golf columnist and radio personality Bill Huffman, it was an excellent opportunity for me to meet and compare notes with other golf writers from around the country and around the world. We were treated royally. The four courses we played were top-notch. The accommodations at the Xona Suites Resort and the banquet dinners we attended were, as the kids of today say, "awesome." The opportunity I had to attend the

Media Classic for the first time was a wonderful experience. I vowed to attend again if invited.

When I received an invitation in 2011 to attend the 12th Annual Media Classic, which was to be held in Mesquite, Nevada in November of 2012, I quickly responded that I would attend. I organized my travel schedule so I could be in Mesquite for the event by changing my original plan to play golf in Nevada and Utah as my first two states. I rerouted my itinerary so they would be the next-to-last two states I would visit. I was happy to do so, anticipating what a grand time it would be playing the courses in Mesquite, located eighty miles north of Las Vegas, and Hurricane, Utah, which is fifty miles northeast of Mesquite and a few miles from St. George, Utah.

After leaving Oregon and spending time visiting friends and relatives in California, I spent three nights at my home in Vista before driving to Las Vegas for a quick, one-night's stay. I decided to spend more than my normal Motel 6 budget and reserved a room in one of Vegas's medium-priced resorts, the Excalibur Hotel and Casino. Once settled in my room, I worked on my script for my Saturday morning radio segment, responded to emails, and then went downstairs to play black jack and pai gow poker. When I got forty dollars ahead, I called it quits and headed to the buffet for a huge meal and a cold beer. I loved having the casino buy me dinner.

The following morning, I drove northeast from Las Vegas to play Coyote Springs Golf Course, a Jack Nicklaus Signature

Design. It was the first course in a long-range plan to build
seven to ten courses and more than 100,000 homes in the
area. The course was an hour's drive from Vegas, including
twenty-eight miles of two-lane road through very desolate
desert. Just as I was ready to turn around, thinking I was lost,
I saw green grass in the distance, so I continued on.

I was glad I did, as the course was outstanding, even in
the cold wind that was blowing. I would like to play Coyote
Springs again on a calm day to see if I could hit more of the
wide fairways, putt better on the big and fast greens, and
avoid some of the water I hit into, which came into play on
twelve holes. I would also like to see if I could steer clear of
the three waste bunkers and the nine fairway and greenside
bunkers I managed to hit into. (There were 117 bunkers on
the course). I did break 100, but barely. Considering the cold,
the wind, and the difficulty of the course—which I played
from the Blues—I was pleased with my score.

After my round, I grabbed a snack and drove to Mesquite
to check into the casual-yet-fashionable Eureka Hotel and
Casino, the first of the two hotels I stayed in while attending
the Media Classic. During my seven days in Mesquite, I also
stayed at a new Holiday Inn Express. Both hotels were excellent and just minutes from the outstanding desert courses in
and around Mesquite. All the courses had dramatic elevation
changes with spectacular views of the surrounding mountains
and valley. Most had wide fairways that wound through high
desert terrain and native grasslands toward large, well-guarded,

sloping greens. All the courses offered great risk/reward options for both low- and high-handicappers.

While attending the Media Classic, I and the other golf writers played five of the more than twenty courses in or near Mesquite. Falcon Ridge, the Palmer and Canyon courses at the Oasis Golf Club, and the Conestoga Golf Club, managed by Troon, were in Mesquite. Our fifth course was Sand Hollow, a twenty-seven hole beauty designed by John Fought located an hour north of Mesquite in Hurricane, Utah and rated Utah's #1 Public Golf Course. All were excellent courses with incredibly scenic holes and desert views.

At the Media Classic, in addition to wonderful golf and camaraderie with fellow golf writers, I had the opportunity to enjoy an extremely humorous and entertaining presentation by former Long-Drive Champion Art Sellenger. He hit drives of over 300 yards with hang time that former Oakland Raider punting great Ray Guy would have been proud of, and he did it with super-short drivers, from tees three feet in the air, and with a putter. He was amazing.

I also attended one day of the three-day International Network of Golf Fall Forum. ING, as it is more commonly known, is an association where golf media and members of the golf industry connect. While in attendance, I listened intently as golf psychology consultant Kevin Roby spoke about how and why confidence, concentration, and emotional control play such a big part in developing successful golf habits and shots. I try to play using what I learned from Dr. Roby.

I thoroughly enjoyed playing golf in and around Mesquite. To my way of thinking, Mesquite is not just a good golf destination, it's an outstanding golf destination, one that should be on every golfer's Bucket List.

When the Media Classic concluded, I was eager to fly to Hawaii, where I was going to finish my year-long odyssey. But first, I had to fly to Little Rock, Arkansas and drive an hour west to meet with rental agent Sherry Spann of ReMax of Hot Springs Village, to talk about renting a home or townhouse in Hot Springs Village.

I came within minutes of missing my Little Rock flight, as there was a serious accident on an overpass on the outskirts of Las Vegas which closed the highway for almost an hour. Thinking I was going to miss my plane, I called the airline and made a reservation on a later flight, but I was forced to cancel my original reservation in order to do so. I was beginning to panic until the cars in front of me began moving. When I got to the airport, my original flight was boarding. I asked to be put back on it. Fortunately, the airline representative was very helpful and was able to get me on the plane, and I flew to Little Rock as scheduled. Thankfully, this was one of only a few difficult experiences I encountered all year.

When I arrived in Hot Springs Village, I called Mrs. Spann to confirm our appointment for the next day. She was to show me a number of rental units that I was considering after viewing them online. I had made the decision to move to Hot Springs Village after carefully considering all my options. (See Week 51 and Beyond). Now it was time to make a decision as to which rental I wanted. Sherry showed me seven or eight rentals, none of which excited me. Then she took me to see a townhouse unit, which in California we would have considered one side of a duplex. She was a good sales person, as she saved the best for last. When I opened the front door and saw forty feet of floor to ceiling windows looking out over a pond and the twelfth green and thirteenth tee on one of the village's eight golf courses, I told Sherry to sign me up.

When I returned to Las Vegas after finalizing the paper work for my new rental, I drove back to Vista and spent two days contacting moving companies for my December move to Hot Springs Village. Then I drove to the San Francisco Bay Area to spend Thanksgiving with friends.

On the Friday after Thanksgiving, my morning flight to Honolulu from San Francisco International Airport took off over "The City by the Bay." With the Golden Gate Bridge in view, we climbed into the sky above the blue Pacific. I was excited. I was actually on my way to play golf in my fiftieth and final state.

Hawaii –
"Waikiki and Jurassic Park"

In 1932, the Matson Navigation Company's S. S. Lurline began carrying passengers between California and Hawaii. In 1939, *Hawaii Calls* began the first of its thirty-six years on radio, broadcasting Hawaiian music live each week from the Moana Hotel on Honolulu's Waikiki Beach. Today, millions of visitors from all over the world travel to Hawaii to relax on its stunning beaches, swim in its warm waters, eat at its world-famous restaurants, take advantage of its wide variety of shopping opportunities, enjoy its beautiful weather, and play golf on its spectacular courses.

In December 2012, I was one of those visitors. When my plane landed in Honolulu on my flight from San Francisco, I realized I was about to spend the final week of my golf odyssey in the Aloha State of Hawaii. What a way to finish!

During my six-day stay in Honolulu on Oahu and my three days at Kapalua on Maui, I had the opportunity to play three totally different courses. On Oahu, I played the Kapolei Golf Club and the Royal Hawaiian, which were owned and operated by Pacific Links International, owners and managers of upscale public and private golf clubs in North America, Asia, and Australia as well as Hawaii. On Maui, I played the Plantation Course at Kapalua.

Kapolei, which was located just a short drive west of Honolulu and the international airport, was a walkable, championship-length course situated on 190 rolling acres on the site of a former sugar cane plantation. It was a favorite course of both locals and visitors. In 2010, it was chosen for a People's Choice Award as the "Best Course on Oahu" by the *Honolulu Star Advertiser.* The pros also liked it. For three years prior to my visit, it had been the site of the Champion Tour's Pacific Links Hawaii Championship and, from 1996 through 2000, it was the site of the LPGA Tour's Ladies Hawaiian Open.

Known for its beautifully landscaped floral gardens, lush Bermuda contoured fairways, and coconut palms that swayed in the trade winds, it had eighty bunkers, five lakes, and water that came into play on eight holes. Although mostly flat with wide landing areas off the tees, quality approach shots were important because of the tropical breezes, the coconut palms, and the numerous, elevated greens, many of which were almost totally surrounded by rippling water in the course's five lakes.

The second course I played on Oahu, the Royal Hawaiian Golf Club, also just a short drive from downtown Honolulu, was in an area where Hawaiian royalty had once lived. Formerly known as Luana Hills Country Club, it was created by Pete Dye and his son Perry in 1993. Its front nine meandered through a gentle valley while the back nine was in the middle of a tropical jungle with native birds and ancient trees that towered more than one-hundred feet tall.

Because of its unspoiled, lush, tropical surroundings, the course, particularly the back nine, had earned the nickname "Jurassic Park." Its incredible back nine got my vote for the most spectacular nine of any of the courses I had played on my "just-about-over" odyssey. I felt as if I was actually in a real-life Jurassic Park, where extinct dinosaurs might suddenly appear. Its hilly terrain and the numerous ravines, ponds, bunkers, and fast, small- to medium-size bentgrass greens made it not only a spectacular course, but a very challenging course.

While in Honolulu, I stayed at the Holiday Inn Waikiki Beachcomber Resort and at the only all-suites hotel in Honolulu, the Embassy Suites Waikiki Beach Walk. Both hotels were conveniently located only minutes from famed Waikiki beach, where I was able to spend some time frolicking in the gentle, rolling surf. Although I had stayed in the Waikiki area several times in the past, I still liked the hustle and bustle of the area.

Whether you have been to Honolulu or will be making your first trip there, be sure to visit the Waikiki area. It's upscale and relaxing, all in one. You can people-watch along

Kalakaua Avenue, dine at casual or elegant restaurants just feet from famed Waikiki Beach, enjoy a Mai Tai while watching the sun slowly sink into the blue Pacific, and, if so inclined, you can shop, shop, shop.

Shopping in Hawaii is quite eclectic. From local crafts to high-end luxury stores, shopping there can be a full-time job. Although I am definitely not a shopper, I can say I thoroughly enjoyed peeking in the windows of the luxury stores on Kalakaua Avenue. My only purchase was a bag of cookies at the Honolulu Cookie Company. They were so good, they didn't make it back to the hotel.

The twenty-five-story, 496-room Holiday Inn Waikiki Beach Resort where I stayed was home to a Jimmy Buffett's Restaurant & Bar, the Honolulu Surfing Museum, and the Magic of Polynesia show starring illusionist John Hirokawa. Modern and recently renovated, the resort was quite nice, with spectacular ocean and city views.

The Embassy Suites Waikiki Beach Walk, my second hotel while in Honolulu, was a 396-room, all-suites resort with one- and two-bedroom suites, each with a separate living room and mini kitchen. Because I took advantage of the hotel's complimentary, cooked-to-order breakfasts and nightly manager's receptions, the kitchen and eating area in my suite was seldom used, except for nightly glasses of wine and my Subway sandwich dinners. Both hotels had pools, restaurants, shops, entertainment, fitness centers, and Wi-Fi, which made my stays very comfortable.

On one of my free days, on the way to spend leisurely sightseeing time at the Polynesian Cultural Center, I stopped at the Dole Plantation for a drink of freshly squeezed, ice-cold pineapple juice. Not too far from the Dole Plantation, I passed Banzai Beach on Oahu's North Shore, where world-class surfers congregate to catch "the big one" on the Banzai Pipeline. At the Polynesian Cultural Center, I watched performers from seven different island cultures perform among the center's forty-two lush, beautiful, and landscaped areas. I had a large and tasty buffet dinner in the Center's Gateway Restaurant and then attended *Ha: Breath of Life*, a dazzling show featuring more than one hundred Polynesian natives, fire knife dancing, special effects, animation, and surround sound.

On one other free day, I also visited the Arizona Memorial and toured the *U.S.S. Missouri* at Pearl Harbor. To my way of thinking, no visit to Honolulu should be complete without a Navy launch ride out across the hallowed waters of Pearl Harbor to visit the Arizona Memorial, the final resting place of 1,102 of the 1,117 sailors and Marines killed on the *Arizona* on December 7, 1941, "the day that will live in infamy."

In order to play my third Hawaiian course, I took a short flight from Honolulu to Maui, rented a car, and headed for Kapalua, where I was scheduled to play the Plantation Course, site of the PGA Tour's winners-only event held each January. Ranked #1 in Hawaii in 2011 by *Golf Digest*, the course had the widest fairways and the largest and fastest greens of any of the previous 140 courses I had played during nearly a year on the road.

I was particularly enthralled by, and enjoyed playing, the downhill, dog-leg left 18th hole, which if played from "the tips" measured a long 685 yards. Having watched on TV as the pros regularly hit 350-yard drives on the course's most memorable hole, I was eager to see what I could do. After slicing my ball into the left rough (I'm a lefty), I connected with a five-iron shot that put me past the 350 mark … nothing to be proud of however as I was playing from the Resort Tees which gave me a 125-yard advantage off the tee.

At Kapalua, I stayed in a fully equipped, one-bedroom Bay Villa with a magnificent view of the nearby island of Molokai. I was able to walk just a few hundred feet to the water's edge to observe crashing waves pounding the rugged coastline. What a way to finish my year-long golf odyssey.

After my three days on Maui, I flew back to Honolulu and caught my scheduled flight back to San Francisco. When I landed, I realized my golf odyssey was over and my goal had been reached. It had been quite an adventure, and one I will always remember.

50-Week,
50-State Wrap Up

My 50-week, 50-state golf odyssey came to an end on December 4, 2012 when I flew back to California from Hawaii after playing golf in my fiftieth state. During my yearlong adventure, I had the opportunity to play 141 different courses, meet wonderful people in every state, and complete an important goal in my life.

I drove 21,503 miles, stayed in 126 different places—including hotels, motels, B&Bs and the homes of friends and relatives—and had the experience of a lifetime. I played in multi-layers of clothes in thirty-four-degree weather and in shorts and golf shirts in 102-degree weather. I played at least two different courses in every state and six different courses in one state.

I played courses from Alaska to Florida, California to Maine. The most northern and southern courses I played were the Eagleglen Golf Course on the Elmendorf-Richardson Joint Military Base in Anchorage, Alaska and Brackenridge in San Antonio, Texas. My lowest score played from at least 5,500 yards on a championship-length course was 76. My highest score was 97 with a number of Xs. My handicap went from 9 to 12.

Everywhere I went, I was asked to name my favorite course. Since I played city, country, mountain, desert, and seashore courses; nine-hole and eighteen-hole courses; public, municipally-owned, and a few private courses, and no two courses were exactly alike, it was impossible to answer which was my favorite course. I truly liked them all.

If you were to ask me about my most memorable courses, I would have to say Chambers Bay, site of the 2015 U.S. Open; the Plantation course at Kapalua on Maui, the venue for the Tournament of Champions Tournament; and the four courses I played in Hot Springs Village, Arkansas.

My 2012 50-week, 50-state golf odyssey was a fun, exciting, and incredible journey … one I will never forget.

WEEK 51 AND BEYOND

"Hot Springs Village"

I moved to Hot Springs Village, Arkansas on December 11 after two months of investigating the area and comparing the pros and cons of moving here or moving back to my former home areas of Vista, California and Walnut Creek, California.

When I compared the quiet, relaxed but active lifestyle of the village, the beauty of the 26,000-acre pine and hardwood forest in which the village is situated, the village's population of only 13,000 residents, the more than 150 active clubs and organizations, the eight championship-length courses (including the private Diamante Country Club), the eleven lakes for boating, swimming, and fishing, the opportunity to rent a three-bedroom, two-bath townhouse on the village's Magellan golf course for $1,100 a month (versus a one-bedroom apartment in Walnut Creek for $1,300 a month), and the realization that I could play golf with a cart on quality, championship-length courses seven days a week for less than $250 a month—the decision wasn't difficult.

Having lived my entire life in California, I decided to lease for one year to see how I liked the village atmosphere and the weather, and to determine how difficult it would be to join golf groups. I quickly felt right at home because of the friendliness of the people I met who were open and helpful to me as a newcomer. Everyone I met had moved to the village not because of a job, but because they wanted to live here. The weather at first did give me some concern because, during the first three weeks I lived in the village, we had two severe thunderstorms, a snow and ice storm, and a tornado warning. Surprisingly, I have adapted well to all three conditions … and I love the four seasons.

My third area of concern was how I was going to meet and join golf groups, since I literally didn't know a soul when I moved to the village. My concerns were short-lived. I spoke with John Paul, the village's Director of Golf at the time, and he suggested I call an avid golfer in the Village by the name of Joe Clem, who it turns out had also lived in Southern California. I called Joe and within three days, I was invited to play in five different groups. Not foursomes, groups. Thanks to Joe's introductions, I now play two or three days a week with great guys in groups of as many as seven or eight foursomes. My wife, Myrna, and I also play with couples' groups periodically on Sundays when we are not traveling.

Hot Springs Village has been described as "a golfer's paradise." I absolutely concur. Because of the myriad of other outdoor activities such as swimming, boating, kayaking, pickle ball, tennis, and hiking, it is also a wonderful place to enjoy outdoor life, even for non-golfers. I love living in Hot Springs Village and am thrilled with my decision to move here. If you are seeking a "golfer's paradise" community with a relaxed yet active lifestyle, come for a visit, but beware … you may never want to leave.

The Odyssey Route

Essentials on my 50-Week, 50-State Golf Odyssey

1. *A Highly Dependable Car.* My car was a 2004 Nissan Maxima with lots of trunk space. It had just over 70.000 miles when I left home, and 91,000 plus miles at the end of my 50 weeks on the road.

2. *A GPS System.* Mine was a portable one, and except for once in West Virginia when it directed me to the wrong side of a lake, it worked fine.

3. *A Good Pillow.* Ever tried sleeping on a different pillow every few nights ... some soft, some hard, some feathers, some foam? I took my pillow from home in order to guarantee I would be sleeping on a comfortable pillow.

4. *A Golf GPS System.* I was given a Golf Buddy voice activated system which I attached to my golf hat. It gave me distances to the front, middle and back of the greens. It had 30,000 courses, including all 141 courses I played. I still use it.

5. *Several Credit Cards.* I charged everything possible in order to get airline miles.

6. *An ATM Card* and a few checks in case I needed cash.

Interesting Numbers

1. Days on the road: 331

2. Miles Driven: 21,503

3. Projected expenses: $13,800

4. Actual expenses: $13,265

5. Self-imposed food/drink budget: $8 to $10/day

6. Courses Played: 141

7. Fewest courses/holes
   played in a state: 2 courses, 22 holes (Louisiana)

8. Most courses/holes
   played in a state: 6 courses, 95 holes (Michigan)

9. Coldest temp at tee-off time: 34 degrees

10. Hottest temp at tee-off time: 96 degrees

11. Rain-out days: 4

12. Days with snow: 0

13. Number of different hotels, motels, etc.:   126

14. Most expensive accommodations: $75/night

15. Cheapest non-comped
    accommodations: $18/night

Index by State

Golfing The U.S.
Reflections on a 50-Week, 50-State Golf Odyssey

I hope you enjoyed your vicarious trip with me around the U.S. If you liked the book, and I sincerely hope you did, please let others know that it can be purchased in one of three ways:

1. *From my publisher CreateSpace.* Going to <u>www.createspace.com/6338675</u> will take you directly to the book. Cost - $14.95 plus shipping and handling.

2. *From Amazon.com.* Going to <u>www.Amazon.com/dp0692731431</u> will take you directly to the book. Cost - $14.95 plus shipping and handling.

3. *From Amazon.com for Kindle.* Cost - $8.95

It is also available via Amazon.com in the UK, France, Italy, Germany and Spain.

Many thanks.

Chuck Miller
The Traveling Guy
Phone: 501-922-1101
Email: Chuck@TheTravelingGuy.com

Charitable Donation

When I traveled to and through all fifty states, I met fascinating people from all walks of life. I was truly impressed by how many were giving back to their communities. Through the sale of my book, I want to also give back.

If your charity or non-profit organization is interested in being considered for a charitable donation, please feel free to contact me at Chuck@TheTravelingGuy.com and let me know why your charity or organization should be recognized for a donation. Please include your name and a telephone number where you can be reached.

Chuck Miller, The Traveling Guy

Made in the USA
San Bernardino, CA
03 May 2017